Breaking the Bondage Barrier – Taking the Limits off God

Steve Sampson

Sovereign World

Sovereign World Ltd
PO Box 777
Tonbridge
Kent
TN11 9XT

Unless otherwise indicated, all Scripture quotations are taken from the New King James Version of the Bible. Copyright © 1983 Thomas Nelson, Inc.

ISBN 1 85240 099 4

Typeset by CRB Typesetting Services, Ely, Cambs.
Printed by R.R. Donnelley & Sons, Co., Harrisonburg, Virginia, USA

Acknowledgements

I would like to express my appreciation to my friends,
Betty and Fred Hicks, for their tireless effort in
editing this manuscript.

Contents

Introduction

In the beginning of our walk with God, we couldn't get enough of our new found freedom of the Holy Spirit and our passionate love relationship with the Lord. We detested our old life of sin (or the religious bondage we were trapped in) and we rejoiced in our relationship with God Who was real and personal, and Who was teaching us and guiding us into freedom.

But bondage is deceiving. While we have tasted glorious portions of the life in the Holy Spirit, we all have a tendency to settle in to suffocating religious form once again.

Instead of longing for the Holy Spirit to stir us, we become uncomfortable and annoyed when He intrudes in our life-style.

Just as the hearts of the children of Israel were inclined to turn back to Egypt at the first momentary encounters with hunger and thirst, many have fled back to the warm womb of their denominational patterns. They've forgotten the miracle of the baptism of the Holy Spirit and the visitation of the Lord.

Many who were once moving in freedom and innocence with the Holy Spirit, are now appallingly content to settle into listless pew-sitting once again. They are no longer provoked that the anointing is missing, and that the church revolves more on personalities of people and human talents and abilities than it does on the freshly breathed oracle and originality of the Spirit of God. We seem almost oblivious to the fact that the Church desperately needs a fresh touch of the Holy Spirit.

Equally, many leaders who once acknowledged a desperate dependence on the Holy Spirit, seem to have learned to function so professionally, that His help is no longer needed.

In this book, I address this compromising spirit that appears to prevail in the church, and how we can prepare for what God has next on His agenda. Truly these are days of preparation for the greatest outpouring of the Holy Spirit that the world has ever known.

Steve Sampson

Chapter 1

How to Create Something out of Nothing

– Every word that God speaks is creative –

*'... even God, who gives life to the dead and **calls those things which do not exist as though they did.***'
(Romans 14:17)

Something was desperately wrong! The pastor looked anxiously at his young wife and mother of their five children who lay delirious with fever, and in much pain. He knew there was no choice but to get her to the hospital.

Soon the paramedics arrived, and the stunned pastor watched them work over his wife lying on the floor of their living room.

'We have a forty-four year old female here, and we are unable to get a pulse,' he heard them say over the transmitter to the medical team at the hospital.

Upon arrival at the hospital, a team of doctors fervently worked over his wife for nearly two hours. Amid all the confusion, it was obvious there was a desperate attempt underway to save her life.

Finally, the pastor could stand it no more. He left the emergency room and walked out into the hospital corridor. An inaudible groan from deep within his being cried out to God.

'Then suddenly', he told me later, 'a most awesome thing happened.'

'Great peace began to come, and then a wonderful unexplainable joy flooded my being.'

He continued.

'Then at the same moment, I had an urge to dance a shuffle. So I did! I danced a little shuffle right there in the hospital corridor.'

God had spoken to this pastor. Not in an audible voice, but with an overwhelming peace and joy. Joy so powerful that he couldn't resist dancing a little shuffle right outside the emergency room where his wife lay struggling between life and death.

Soon the doctor came out to report to him. 'We're sorry,' the physician told him, 'your wife has severe pancreatitis. We've done all we can. She may not live more than a few hours.'

For the next two days, he continued to hear the same prognosis. Every few hours, he was told there was little hope.

On the third day, the surgeon in charge called him into his office and showed him a diagram of her condition. As he explained in detail, he told him that the only other two patients he had treated with this condition had died from it. Six out of seven patients with this condition, who had been treated in this same hospital, had also died. He gave him little hope.

The condition of pancreatitis was caused by a gallstone that had slipped through and lodged in the duct where the pancreatic fluid came through. As a result, the unreleased fluid came back upon the pancreas and the pancreas began devouring itself. Most people (as my friend was informed) don't survive with this condition, and those who do, end up with diabetes or severe medical problems.

For two weeks, various doctors related the same prognosis to him. 'It's touch and go,' they would say, 'your wife may not live through this.'

The Creative Word of God

Here is the exciting part! During the first few hours of this life and death crisis, the Spirit of God had spoken to this pastor.

Yet nothing happened immediately. In fact, for the next thirteen days, his wife remained in a 'touch and go' battle for her life. But on the fourteenth day, she was released from the hospital with a clean bill of health and with no medication required. No diabetes. No medical problems. She was completely well!

Although God had spoken to this pastor, the situation didn't instantly change. In fact, it looked worse! But God knows the end from the beginning.

At the beginning of the crisis, the sweet Holy Spirit communicated to him by giving Him a joyful assurance, **a word from His mouth** that his wife would be okay. Although many medical accounts came forth to the contrary for several days, God's Word proved true. He does not lie, nor does He give false hope.

The Last Chapter God

When the Holy Spirit spoke to this pastor, He gave Him a concrete word of glorious assurance that carried him through the ordeal. The peace and joy that God gave was describing the outcome of the crisis. God often speaks in this manner. He declares a promise to us that 'guarantees' what the outcome will be. He doesn't promise that there will not be conflict or contrary circumstances in between, but he **does** promise that it will end in victory.

Hearing from God in such a crisis is like reading the last chapter of a book **first**, and then reading the beginning of the book, secondly. All the while you are reading the book, you already know how it is going to end. You read with an assurance of how it is going to turn out. The peace of God at all times rules and reigns in your heart. Although your mind may question and analyze, the peace of God doesn't lie.

> '*And let the peace (soul harmony which comes) from Christ rule (act as umpire continually) in your hearts – deciding and settling with finality all questions that arise in your minds...*'

(Colossians 3:15 Amplified)

When the Lord spoke to Moses and told him to send spies into Canaan to see what the land was like, He never once mentioned the giants that lived there. The presence of giants was irrelevant to the mind of God, because He had **already** given the land to the Israelites. He had already determined the 'last chapter.'

God doesn't care what circumstances dictate. He calls forth into being that which doesn't **yet exist** by examination of the natural eye.

God is a last chapter God. He declares to us the victory **before** we see the manifestation. But as we receive that personal word of promise from God, we can walk through any crisis or conflict with assurance and victory. We can act as if it is already so, because it **is** so!

Man was meant to live in a continual state of fellowship and communication with his Father God. We were created to live a life of listening to the Holy Spirit. As Christians we have learned this truth; when God talks, things happen.

The Creative Flow in Your Inner Man

There seems to be so little teaching or preaching in this area, but when you begin to recognize that the creative flow of God is **in** your inner man, awesome things begin to take place.

On the last day of the Feast of Tabernacles, Jesus stood up and cried out,

> *'If anyone thirsts, let him come to Me and drink. **He who believes in Me**, as the Scripture has said, out of his heart (innermost being) will flow rivers of living water.'*
>
> (John 7:37–39)

Notice He doesn't limit the flow of living water to special people, or to the priesthood but to *'He who believes in Me.'*

Paul prayed a potent prayer for the Christians at Ephesus.

> *'That He would grant you, according to the riches of His glory, to be strengthened with might **through His Spirit in the inner man**.'*
>
> (Ephesians 3:16)

The writer of Hebrews rebukes them for not **exercising** their inner man:

> *'For though by this time you ought to be teachers, you need someone to teach you **again** the first principles of the oracles of God ... those who by **reason of use have their senses exercised** to discern both good and evil.'*
>
> (Hebrews 5:12–14)

God has placed the creative flow of the Holy Spirit in the inner man of the believer.

No longer do we just pray, we have come to realize we can pray with creative power and effectiveness. Because the prophetic and creative word of the Lord is in us, mountains must move!

Recently I was asked to pray for a precious woman who had just undergone medical tests. The doctor had told her that surgery was inevitable, and the next day they were going to run a few more tests to determine the extent of surgery needed.

On Sunday morning, the pastor asked me to come up front to lay hands on her, as she was battling much fear. He had caught me off guard, and I certainly didn't feel very anointed or spiritual, but as we began to pray, I felt that familiar creative voice of the Lord rise up within me. I stopped praying and told her what I was hearing from the Spirit. 'Tomorrow when the doctors examine you, they are going to find absolutely nothing wrong, and send you home.'

She looked at me very surprised, and frankly I was surprised too. In fact, later, because the word of the Lord had come so effortlessly, I had to battle thoughts that I had made it all up.

However, a little over twenty-four hours later, I received a call from the pastor telling me that they had run more tests on the lady, and had found nothing, and had sent her home.

This is normal Christianity! It is normal to **hear** from God, and to have a creative word of the Lord in your mouth.

Jesus **always** spoke the creative word. It didn't matter what the outward condition was. When He told ten lepers to show themselves to the priests (Luke 17), there was creative power in that word, because the leprosy was gone before they could find the priests.

Jesus spoke to another leper who desired healing,

> *'"I am willing; be cleansed." And immediately he was cleansed.'*
>
> (Matthew 8:3)

The centurion requested Jesus to speak the word for his ailing servant,

> *'But only speak a word, and my servant will be healed.'*
> (Matthew 8:8)

Jesus spoke the creative word.

> *'... "Go your way; and as you have believed, so let it be done for you." And his servant was healed that same hour.'*
>
> (Matthew 8:13)

To the paralytic, He spoke,

> *"Arise, take up your bed, and go to your house."*
> (Matthew 9:6)
> *'And he arose and departed to his house.'*
>
> (vs. 7)

Over and over Jesus ministered to people through the creative word of the Lord.

> *'He sent His word and healed them, and delivered them from their destructions.'*
>
> (Psalm 107:20)

Don't be in Bondage to the Spectacular

By far, the greatest hindrance in hearing from God, is the spectacular. There seems to be an unspoken concept in the minds of believers, that any time God speaks, it will be sensational and grandiose. But if you are waiting for God to be spectacular, you probably won't hear Him.

One reason that God will not communicate to us through the spectacular (and there are exceptions) is that it would take no faith on our part. Without faith it is impossible to please God (Hebrews 11:6).

It takes faith to pay attention to the still, small voice of the Holy Spirit within your own spirit.

God is always talking. The problem is that we haven't understood that He desires to talk to us **now**, while we are on this earth, and in everyday situations. If you are His child, the Holy Spirit will communicate to you. You don't have to wait until some day in heaven to become intimate in your fellowship with Him.

Jesus is our example. He had ears to hear what the Father was saying. The pivotal point of His ministry was living in a continual recognition and awareness of what the Father was doing and saying. We too, are to live in this realm. To be effective for God, we have to recognize what He is doing in our lives, and **agree** with it. Nowhere does the Scripture tell us to work for God, but work with Him. And He will then work with us.

> '*And they went out and preached everywhere, the Lord working with them and confirming the word through the accompanying signs.*'
>
> (Mark 16:20)

The Devil is an Abortionist

It is obvious to me now, after many years of walking with the Lord, what ploys the devil uses. The devil uses any means to obstruct or abort the flow of the Holy Spirit in the life of the believer. If the enemy of your soul can keep you from hearing the voice of the Lord, his attack has been successful.

That is why Christians must be on guard against **all** the wiles of the devil.

Whether the attack comes in the form of discouragement,

depression, feelings of rejection, low self-esteem, or other blatant lies, the strategy of the devil is the same. His attempt is to try to keep you from staying in the stream of that glorious communication and creative flow of the Holy Spirit. All these areas of attack and discouragement are the enemy attempting to bring about an abortion of the creative word of God that He is speaking to your spirit.

The voice of the Lord is not intermittent. Our hearing is intermittent. God desires that we resist the ploys and distractions of the enemy and abide in His presence. He is a twenty-four hour Holy Spirit. He abides in the believer.

The Analytical Mind

The analytical mind is the greatest hindrance to the creative flow of the Holy Spirit in the life of the believer. Keeping it in subjection to the Holy Spirit seems to be the biggest struggle we have as we desire to hear from God.

We all have a tendency to analyze things. After all, from kindergarten up, we are taught to think for ourselves. But God's Word is perfect and pure, and doesn't need analyzing.

When we analyze, we are usually trying to figure out how God is going to solve a specific problem. But the good news is, listening to God will bring far more results than analyzing Him. God can speak a word to you in the situation that will be creative and bring wondrous results.

The Key to the Creative Flow of God is Listening

There are many exciting aspects regarding the baptism in the Holy Spirit. But the most life-changing area for me has been that I began to have daily communion and communication with the Holy Spirit. People often make the prayer language (praying in tongues) a complicated issue, but really it is very simple. From the first day that a pastor prayed for me and I spoke in my new language of tongues, I began to have experiences of **hearing** the Holy Spirit. There is something so indescribably wonderful when the Holy Spirit is released in each of us. He enables us to communicate with God in a more intimate way. Some say that the prayer language is one of the least gifts, yet in some ways it is the most important. The prayer language can be likened as a key to a house. A key only has one function; to open the door. Yet what good is an entire house if you can't get the door open? But with the key, small as it is, an entire dimension is opened up to you.

To this day, when I pray in tongues even briefly, my spirit will immediately begin to hear from the Holy Spirit. What higher level of experience could anyone desire, beyond hearing from God, Himself?

> *'For he who speaks (prays) in a tongue does not speak to men but to God, for no one understands him; however, in the spirit he speaks mysteries.'*
>
> (1 Corinthians 14:2)

God's Creative Word is Perpetual

A word from God will have a far more lasting impact than any material blessing that could ever come your way.

Our vision tends to be short-sighted. We see only the small picture, namely how we can get our immediate needs met. But God sees the far greater picture.

A perfect example of this is when God sent Elijah to a certain widow at Zarephath.

> *'Arise, go to Zarephath, which belongs to Sidon, and dwell there. See, I have commanded a widow there to provide for you.'*
>
> (1 Kings 17:9)

God sees the end from the beginning in all matters that concern us. It is interesting that He told Elijah that He had already commanded a widow to provide for him. It is not clear whether God had already spoken to the widow, or if God knew her heart and knew she would be responsive to the word of the prophet.

The first thing that Elijah does upon arriving at the city is to ask the widow for a cup of water.

'So he arose and went to Zarephath. And when he came to the gate of the city, indeed a widow was there gathering sticks. And he called to her and said, "Please bring me a little water in a cup, that I may drink."'

(vs. 10)

She immediately obeyed. As she obeyed, he called to her again.

'And as she was going to get it, he called to her and said, "Please bring me a morsel of bread in your hand."'

(vs. 11)

God always speaks to us with a verb. He intends to get us moving. Elijah (representing the Lord), asks for water, which is in the realm of the possible, but as she begins to move in obedience, he calls out to her to bring a morsel of bread, which is the realm of the impossible.

Then she explains her predicament, a situation that Elijah no doubt fully knew by the Spirit. He knew she was in an impossible situation, but he was sent to her by God, in order to give her the creative word, so she might **be released** in the creative flow of God. If we disobey God and don't yield to the Spirit, we could be responsible for the creative flow not being released in someone else.

'Then she said, "As the Lord your God lives, I do not have bread, only a handful of flour in a bin, and a little oil in a jar; and see, I am gathering a couple of sticks that I may go in and prepare it for myself and my son, that we may eat it, and die."'

(vs. 12)

Note the creative word that Elijah speaks to this widow. He first tells her not to fear. In the Scripture, any time God speaks and says, 'Do not fear,' something awesome is getting ready to happen. God commands us not to fear, because fear will paralyze and hinder us from embracing the oracle God is speaking.

> *'And Elijah said to her, "Do not fear; go and do as you have said, but make me a small cake from it first, and bring it to me; and afterward make some for yourself and your son."'*

(vs. 13)

Now notice the creative oracle of the Lord.

> *'For thus says the Lord God of Israel: "The bin of flour shall not be used up, nor shall the jar of oil run dry, until the day the Lord sends rain on the earth."'*

(vs. 14)

The promise was for an **endless** supply. God gave a perpetual word; a word that would flow until the famine was long ended.

Now observe what God did **not** say. My natural mind, like yours, would want to provide for her needs in some way. We might choose to raise money for her, or to organize some type of 'Operation Help Her,' and have a semi-truck load of bread and oil sent in.

But if we organized such a task, it would only be temporary. The semi-truck load would eventually run out, or it could get bugs in it, or be stolen, or even seized by the government.

But He gave her something **better** than a truck load of goods. He gave her a perpetual promise, a promise that the bin of flour and the jar of oil would not run out!

A Word from God is endless

We usually think in limitation. For example, when we have a need, our analytical minds immediately go to work thinking of a way to get our need met.

But what would you rather have? A solution to the immediate crisis facing you, or a perpetual word from the Lord?

If you were having difficulty, and someone came and handed you a large check, you, like me, would probably

21

rejoice. But before long that check would be used to pay the bills at hand, and we would be back in the situation we were before – in need of another check.

But God doesn't give you the check. He does far better! He gives you a living and creative word, that He will be faithful to provide all your needs.

A friend of mine who has written a number of popular gospel songs, and now travels the world singing, was in such a situation.

This man is so refreshing, because he has always refused to appeal to people or even hint about his financial needs. Never once has he made an appeal for finances.

After walking faithfully before God in this realm, and choosing to let God be His source, God sent someone to him with a prophetic word. The word was, 'You will never have a financial need in your ministry again.'

This word was prophesied over ten years ago, and God has proven Himself over and over to my friend.

Now if the Lord had moved on someone to simply give him a check for ten thousand dollars, that would have been exciting. However, as wonderful as that sounds, that money would have been spent long ago.

But God gave him something far greater; a promise that he would have an endless and perpetual supply.

When God Speaks, Things Most Always Look Contrary

God couldn't care less what the natural situation dictates. He is creative, and one word from His mouth guarantees a glorious outcome, no matter what the circumstances.

The first thing to do when you face a crisis is pray. Then listen. Then pray some more. Then listen some more. God will give **you** a word that will take you through the crisis. His word to you will be a word you can stand on because it will be a promise of the outcome of the situation.

While we were pastoring in Texas, a wonderful family moved to our city. They had recenty sold their home in another city, and felt that the Lord was directing them to our city. They were so happy to be a part of our church family. For the next year and a half the Lord did many wonderful things in their spiritual lives. In fact, they felt as if God had appointed those eighteen months just for their spiritual growth and refreshing.

The problem was, that although spiritually it was an oasis for this family, the man encountered great difficulty finding a good paying job. They struggled a great deal financially and eventually spent the entire equity from their former home. We prayed a great deal with them about it, and each time we prayed, the Lord would give a knowledge that He was aware of their financial need and would take care of it. Looking back, we can see that God was not merely implying that things would work out okay, but He was, in fact, speaking a creative oracle.

Finally a promising job opportunity opened up in Houston, and they moved there. Then after living in Houston and renting a number of months, a man approached them. 'I feel like the Lord is telling me to give you this extra home I have,' he told them. This home had a large equity in it, and he signed the title over to our friends. The remainder owed required only a modest monthly payment that they could easily afford. The Lord gave them back more than double what they had lost. Today they are in full-time ministry.

Yes, it looked contrary at first. But the creative word of the Lord defies all obstacles.

We Were Created to Live by Listening

It isn't enough to have the Bible memorized. We must also **hear** the Holy Spirit. When He speaks, creative life issues forth.

> *'Man shall not live by bread alone, but by every word that proceeds from the mouth of God.'*
>
> (Matthew 4:4)

Numerous times the Holy Spirit has spoken in meetings that a married couple who were present had not been able to conceive, but soon would. We have heard many testimonies from these couples who had been given no hope from the medical field that they would ever be able to conceive a child. It is always exciting to later see with our eyes, them holding the evidence. God always fulfils the Word He speaks.

Oftentimes in meetings the Lord will indicate His desire to heal skin conditions. It is exciting when people can immediately reveal and testify (with positive evidence) that the creative word has gone forth and removed a lump, or rash during the service. Numerous women have reported a lump on the breast dissolving (after leaving the meeting momentarily and making a quick examination) usually only minutes after the Holy Spirit has spoken that He is working such a miracle.

When the Holy Spirit talks, His words are creative. It is exciting when a person with a deaf ear can suddenly begin hearing out of that ear again, or a person with crippling arthritis can freely move (without pain) that area of his body where the pain once was.

It is easy to believe that Jesus healed people as He ministered nearly two thousand years ago, but He has also put a creative word in the mouth of believers. As we are obedient to speak what **He** puts in our mouths, the word will produce results.

> *'So shall My word be that goes forth from My mouth; It shall not return to Me void, but it shall accomplish what I please, and it shall prosper in the thing for which I sent it.'*

> (Isaiah 55:11)

Every word that God speaks is creative. Tune in!

Chapter 2

No Regard for the Holy Spirit

– The Holy Spirit is the most accessible, yet the least utilized Person in many churches –

> *'And my speech and my preaching were not with persuasive words of human wisdom, but in **demonstration of the Spirit and of power**, that your faith should not be in the wisdom of men but in the power of God.'*
>
> (1 Corinthians 2:4–5)

During the past decade many of the rapidly growing churches have assimilated a new policy in order to 'minister' to the masses.

This concept is especially becoming popular and accepted for the Sunday morning services. The strategy is this; rather than it being a particularly spiritual service, with the Holy Spirit initiating things, some pastors have chosen instead to engage in more of a professional production.

In the name of reaching their community and not offending potential new members or converts, scores of the mega churches and the potential mega churches have embraced this strategy.

The Sunday morning production necessitates that there be no Holy Spirit manifestations such as prophecy or messages in tongues, no personal prophetic ministry or any yieldedness in the area of divine healing and miracles. Such 'things' should be reserved for other meetings.

The strategy is to put forth the most professional and polished production possible, in order to influence the multitudes. This includes professional musical performances, drama, and non-offensive preaching.

My heart grieves over this. Why leave out the Holy Spirit when He is the only One who can convict of sin and convert hearts?

In the book of Acts, multitudes were not added to the church because of man's professional capabilities, but rather because of powerfully anointed preaching, and the power of God flowing through the apostles.

> *'Then those who gladly received his word were baptized; and that day about three thousand souls were added to them.'*

(Acts 2:41)

> *'Then fear came upon every soul, and many wonders and signs were done through the apostles.'*

(Acts 2:43)

Only the Spirit Gives Life

As a minister, I have always prayed a specific prayer. My prayer is that any time I am preaching, teaching or ministering, the Lord would cause **life** to flow through me. The essence of true ministry is life. The only true life source is the Spirit of God. And, we stand in a time when it is paramount that men make room for the Spirit to move. The only chance for the hearts of people to be truly converted is through the moving of the Holy Spirit.

A popular Scripture is from 2 Corinthians 3:17 *'Now the Lord is the Spirit; and where the Spirit of the Lord is, there is liberty.'* But a more accurate translation of that verse is **'Where the Spirit is Lord, there is liberty.'**

It is only the moving of the Holy Spirit that brings results. And, the Spirit will not move unless He is given the freedom to be **Lord** in that setting. Anything else that we label as the activity of the Holy Spirit is only a man-made substitute.

26

No Regard for the Holy Spirit

*'Not by might nor by power, **but by My Spirit**, says the Lord of hosts.'*

(Zechariah 4:6)

There are a number of reasons that pastors do not let the Holy Spirit move in their midst.

1. Fear that Holy Spirit activity will turn off the sinner. Will His manifestations offend the sinner? Absolutely not! This view is simply a lack of faith. In fact, those in charge are exhibiting more faith in human flesh than in the power of the Spirit. The reason being that there is more regard for man's way of doing things and making them **palatable** so no visitor, prominent person, or good tither will be offended. It is sad that these leaders find the actual manifestation of the Holy Spirit offensive. How ridiculous! We're interacting with God, the author of all salvation, and the only true soul-winner.

The main reason a sinner normally attends church is to seek and search for more than he presently has. In his world, everyone is compromising. Everyone is living a lie. No one needs more exposure to the life of the Spirit than he does. Yet sometimes pastors think they are doing God a favor to keep the meeting palatable so absolutely no one is offended. Let's face reality! People need to see the power and demonstration of the Spirit of God in action. Let the world compromise and dilute the truth. But we must let the Lord be Lord in our midst.

We **preach** a gospel that is supernatural, yet we won't let God be supernatural. Why not just let God act like God?

'For our gospel did not come to you in word only, but also in power, and in the Holy Spirit and in much assurance . . .'

(1 Thessalonians 1:5)

2. Former experiences with flakiness exhibited. As so many of the fastest growing churches have become more and more void of a Spirit-controlled atmosphere, I have questioned pastors about this. The answer is invariably the same. They repeatedly indicated to me that they have had bad experiences in the past with flaky prophecies through people with more zeal than wisdom, so they have chosen to have nothing at all. Although I can surely empathize with them on this subject, I do not agree with their logic. Their logic equals someone who has been handed some counterfeit twenty-dollar bills, and therefore, refuses to have anything more to do with money.

It is obvious that this is what some classic pentecostal pastors have done. In fact, numerous pastors I have conversed with are quick to relate misuses and excesses in the gifts of the Spirit. Years ago, when they were teen-agers growing up in the church, they witnessed some of these excesses and abuses, and 'vowed' never to let it happen in their ministry.

Fear is the culprit. Fear of someone getting in the flesh, and fear of people being offended. But it is a feeble excuse to have to account for before God someday, why the Holy Spirit wasn't allowed to move in the flock where God placed you. 'I was afraid, so I closed the door to the Holy Spirit.'

> *'And I was afraid, and went and hid your talent in the ground. Look, there you have what is yours.'*
> (Matthew 25:25)

If we do not regard the Person of the Holy Spirit in our meetings, what do we have left? What we have left is palatable Christianity that tiptoes around the real Person of the Holy Spirit. We have a substitute of talent, competence and professionalism in place of Holy Ghost power.

Talking with some of the younger leaders who are more of a product of the Charismatic Movement, many have a quick recall of someone who gave a prophecy that was way off-base and how it inflicted potential injury in someone's life.

I believe this is a total cop-out, and typified as 'throwing out the baby with the bath water.' Anyone who has been in leadership very long has seen embarrassing excesses, but that is no reason to put the Holy Spirit on hold.

How rational is it to 'tell' the Holy Spirit not to manifest

Himself, based on the premise that someone might step a little out of order or get in the flesh?

What is especially sad is that leaders choose to sacrifice the Holy Spirit, Himself, for the sake of not offending anyone.

We desperately need to witness the manifestations (expressions) of the Holy Spirit, Himself.

3. The lack of control. Leaders must become accustomed to letting go of the control of the meeting and letting it be totally turned over to the Holy Spirit. While this seems frustrating to man, it gives the Spirit, Himself, room to function and manifest Himself. Too many leaders obstruct the manifestation of the Spirit by fighting for control of the meeting. In their ignorance they do not realize they are fighting against God. What a shame that they've never over-come this obstacle and still entertain fear. Their fear is usually manifested in their own overbearing presence in the meeting, and no one feels free to give forth something the Holy Spirit is giving him or her. However, this is where faith comes in. Faith involves taking a risk. The risk is trusting God to manifest Himself – and not worrying about the consequences.

An old saying is 'It's better to have a little wildfire, than no fire at all.'

These leaders usually control or manipulate a meeting by intimidation. But leaders must make known to their fol-lowers that people are not only free to step out in faith and exercise in the gifts of the Spirit, but they are also free to make mistakes.

4. Fear of taking risks. If there is a synonym to faith, it is taking risks! Risk-taking has not been a popular sport in Christian circles. However, I am always reminded of the Scripture, *'But without faith it is impossible to please Him'* (Hebrews 11:6). God didn't say that it was 'more difficult' or 'it takes more time and effort' but that without faith it is **impossible** to please God.

Frankly, I think most people suffer from a serious case of the fear of man. *'The fear of man brings a snare'* (Proverbs 29:25). We need to pray for deliverance.

The world understands risk-taking. It is a risk to drive in

traffic. It is a risk to eat in a restaurant. It is a risk to get married. It is a risk to have children. It is a risk to start a business. The world is full of risks.

But in the life of the Holy Spirit, we 'teach' people to be careful, to be conservative, to think 'normally' and the underlying motive for teaching people such things is that we are afraid of what people will think. We build parameters that are 'acceptable to society' around people. If we are honest with ourselves, we want the world to think highly of us. But then I'm reminded of Jesus' words,

> *'Woe to you when all men speak well of you, for so did their fathers to the false prophets.'*
>
> (Luke 6:26)

My wife likes to refer to those that are too concerned about the opinions of people as those who walk the 'safe and narrow.'

Following the Holy Spirit is not risk-free living!

5. No regard for the Holy Spirit. Now we address the most serious area. If there is anyone in the universe who requires respect, it is the Holy Spirit. Yet I meet few people who really show respect and regard for Him. Our attitude is far too casual when we make mention of Him.

Again, we fear man whom we see, more than we fear God whom we cannot see. God is dealing with His church about this commonness with which we regard the Holy Spirit. We must be careful to esteem, respect and revere His presence.

Leadership has been guilty of not teaching people to show more respect and honor to the person of the Spirit.

When the Holy Spirit is moving in a meeting, people should be taught not to move around, not to get up and go to the drinking fountain, or the restroom. Such movement is extremely disrespectful to the Holy Spirit. Overall there is a casualness and lack of respect for His presence. This general lack of reverence and awe, certainly contributes to the reason we do not experience more activity of the Holy Spirit in our midst.

6. An unwillingness to provide an environment to learn.

During our years of pastoring, the Lord continually instructed my wife and me not only to encourage people to obey God, but to provide an environment conducive to doing that. Plainly, we encouraged people to bring forth any utterance or manifestation the Lord gave to them, as long as it was with humility and a teachable spirit.

The Lord revealed to us during those years that it was okay to have a 'classroom' atmosphere. After all, people have to have the opportunity to exercise the gifts of the Holy Spirit.

The exciting thing was that the words of prophecy that came forth through the congregation, oftentimes accurately expressed the identical subject matter that the Lord had given me to preach. This was always especially reassuring to me, because those who yielded to the prophetic utterances had no way of knowing what the Lord had directed me to preach. It got to the point where I could hardly wait until the worship service began and the Spirit began moving, so that I could hear the confirmation given prophetically of what God had given me in the secret place.

Additionally, people would receive awesome words from the Lord concerning direction for others, and for their own lives.

Equally amazing was the reaction of newcomers, and yes, even sinners at the meetings where the gifts of Holy Spirit always functioned. I would frequently hear feedback such as, 'I didn't understand everything, but I felt something I've never felt before.' Or, 'I felt so loved, and so close to God.'

When the day came that the Lord told us to step out in faith and resign the pastorate, it was a tearful time. As my wife and I stood before the congregation of people there in Beaumont, Texas, it was evident in eight short years, how much the people had matured in their ability to hear from the Spirit.

After I shared with them how God had spoken to us in a sovereign way and had told us that we were to resign the pastorate and begin travelling, a number of the saints began to minister to my wife and me prophetically. Their ministry to us came forth with great maturity and accuracy. They prophesied things to us that only we and God knew. Many of the prophetic words are still coming to pass years later.

Christians need a place to exercise the gifts of the Holy Spirit within them. Why can't the church be a classroom for learning how to operate in the Holy Spirit? The only way to exercise the gift of prophecy, or word of knowledge, wisdom, or gifts of healing is by beginning to function in those gifts. Learning comes best by **doing**.

If there is flakiness, why can't it simply be corrected in love, rather than using it as an excuse to shut down the activity of the Holy Spirit altogether?

People need to be given the freedom to exercise the gifts of the Spirit in the house of God where there is authority and correction available. The local church can be a working model and a showcase of what God wants to do on a larger scale.

The more the presence of the Lord is allowed to manifest, the more He will be recognized by individuals, and because of the increased intensity of His presence, there will develop a fear and reverence that will grip the individuals' hearts.

> *'Be silent, all flesh, before the Lord, for He is aroused from His holy habitation.'*
>
> (Zechariah 2:13)

7. *Worship services suitable to the sinner.* If there is ever a top priority needed in a church, it is having a worship leader who is sensitive to the Holy Spirit. Sadly, this position is often filled by a song-leader and not a worship leader (there is a big difference) and therefore, the services are continually victimized and robbed of the true moving of the Holy Spirit.

An insensitive song leader will intrusively break the flow of the Spirit. His nervousness and lack of maturity will lead him to interrupt at any pause in the service. At that point, he will quickly quench the Spirit by introducing another song, or throw cold water on the swelling move of the Holy Spirit by trying to exhort on something. By then the Spirit is so offended and obviously unwelcome that His presence is greatly diminished in the service.

Pastors and leaders are responsible in finding a worship leader who can lead the people into the presence of God, not into a palatable plateau of religious calisthenics.

What is often the case, however, is the pastor is too preoccupied to recognize the need for true spiritual worship, so he nonchalantly selects a talented song leader, who is just as bound with human respect as he is. A tremendously gifted and talented musician has just replaced the Holy Spirit.

But let's face facts. **Talent and competence cannot bring forth the Spirit**.

The most amazing thing to me has always been the visitors' (especially sinners) attitude toward worship. When we were in the pastorate, we always encouraged (and still do) the singing in the Spirit. After several choruses, we encouraged the people to worship, by not singing any specific tune, but to make melody in their own hearts, and sing in their prayer language or in their own words, melodious praise to God.

Rarely would we ever hear any negative reaction to this type of worship. If we did, it was usually by a religious legalist.

Almost without fail we would hear visitors remark how they thought it was so beautiful and how they **felt** the presence of the Lord as people entered into worship. Although visitors didn't always understand everything that went on, they couldn't deny the authenticity of the presence of the Lord.

In fact, it is true worship which causes the presence of the Lord to manifest. I might point out that true worship is 'birthed' in individuals by the Holy Spirit. It is not learned out of a book or by attending a worship conference. Those desiring to enter in must make an effort and a discipline to yield to the Lord until He births true worship in them.

> *'But You are holy, who inhabits (enthroned in) the praises of Israel.'*
>
> (Psalm 22:3)

The presence of the Lord will quickly reveal to any person

if his heart is right with God. Those He is trying to woo to Himself will not be able to deny His presence. Even if they get angry, they will know they've been in the presence of the Lord.

Let's not forget, it is only the presence of the Lord Himself Who can do a work in any heart.

8. *Not willing to pay the price.* There is a price to pay to do things God's way. It has to do with laying our own agendas at the feet of Jesus. It has to do with waiting on God, even for days or weeks or months, until He reveals His choice as worship leader, elder, or various other offices in the church. Many pastors are far too impulsive when it comes to appointing people. Actually, it is not the pastor's job to appoint anyone; his part is to recognize those whom God is putting His hand upon for that office. Tragically, many pastors who deeply desire to do things God's way, still submit to pressure from the people.

The best stand for any pastor to take is to watch the cream rise to the top. If people get restless, the pastor must have enough willingness and fortitude to wait upon God and do it God's way. There are really no options.

Saul wasn't willing to pay the price to wait for Samuel to arrive, so he went ahead and offered his own sacrifice. This isn't in Scripture by accident. This is an extremely important principle and a warning to us. Even when our flesh gets frustrated (and it will) we are not to move ahead of God.

> *'Then he waited seven days, according to the time set by Samuel. But Samuel did not come to Gilgal; and the people were scattered from him.'*
>
> (1 Samuel 13:8)

> *'So Saul said, "Bring a burnt offering and peace offerings here to me." And he offered the burnt offering'*
>
> (vs. 9)

> *'Now it happened, **as soon** as he had finished presenting the burnt offering, that Samuel came; and Saul went out to meet him, that he might greet him.'*
>
> (vs. 10)

'And Samuel said, "What have you done?" Saul said, "When I saw that the people were scattered from me, and that you did not come within the days appointed, and that the Philistines gathered together at Michmash,"'

(vs. 11)

'Then I said, "The Philistines will now come down on me at Gilgal, and I have not made supplication to the Lord." Therefore I felt compelled, and offered a burnt offering.'

(vs. 12)

The 'Do Somethings'

That is the problem. Saul felt compelled. He just **had** to do something. This is so true today. If leaders do not exhibit a willingness to wait on God, they will always **feel compelled** to do something. I call it the disease of the 'do somethings.' This fleshly, and man-obligated impulsiveness has to be crucified, if we desire to be used by God.

The penalty to Saul was great. He failed the test. God removed him, and sought out a man after His own heart.

'And Samuel said to Saul, "You have done foolishly. You have not kept the commandment of the Lord your God, which He commanded you. For now the Lord would have established your kingdom over Israel forever. But now your kingdom shall not continue. The Lord has sought for Himself a man after His own heart, and the Lord has commanded him to be commander over His people, because you have not kept what the Lord commanded you."'

(vs. 13–14)

Just as Samuel delayed, so too, God always seems slow. But God isn't slow; He just isn't bound to our time schedule! He has His own schedule. The question is, are we willing to pay the price to wait upon Him for it?

When Saul realized that Samuel wasn't going to arrive on schedule, he took matters into his own hands. This is where many ministers compromise.

Here is where the problem lies. Most ministers **do pray**, but they don't pray with an attitude to wait upon God. They don't want their own agenda interrupted. When they don't 'hear anything' right away, they assume it is okay to go ahead with their plans. This is nothing but presumption, and the consequences can be severe. The consequences for Saul were plain and simple. God would remove his kingdom from him. The plans for God to establish Saul's kingdom over Israel forever were aborted.

> *'Keep back Your servant also from **presumptuous** sins; Let them not have dominion over me. Then I shall be blameless. And I shall be innocent of great transgression.'*
>
> (Psalm 19:13)

Waiting on God is a great discipline to the flesh. The flesh wants to go ahead and get things done. Those yielding to the flesh will wait on God as long as He abides by their time schedule, but when He doesn't, they just shrug their shoulders and go ahead with their plans.

The problem here is more severe than it appears. Saul was a type of those who are not willing to pay the price. Doing things God's way means that our agendas must be laid at His feet.

Saul felt pressured, as many leaders do today. The prevailing attitude is 'We've got to do something.'

Pastors with this attitude are usually gifted administrators, but Saul probably was too. In order to please God and obey Him fully, we must be worshippers. The Father seeks for worshippers.

> *'But the hour is coming, and now is, when the true worshippers will worship the Father in spirit and truth; for the Father is seeking such to worship Him.'*
>
> (John 4:23)

True worshippers are willing to pay the price to know the heart of God. Paying the price means you may be misunderstood. How foolish it appears to the flesh to have to say such things as, 'I haven't heard from the Lord about that yet,' or 'God hasn't released me yet.'

Those who fit the Saul pattern will laugh and mock at these expressions. They will even make light out of such convictions to justify their own conscience which is saying, 'Compromiser, compromiser.'

Chapter 3

The Limitlessness of God

*– The **only** thing that limits God, is our own low level of expectation –*

> *'Now to Him who is able to do exceedingly abundantly above all that we ask or think, according to the power that works in us.'*
>
> (Ephesians 3:20)

I was conducting a men's retreat in southern Illinois a few years ago. At the end of the first evening's teaching, the Holy Spirit began to speak to me words of knowledge of things He desired to do that night. The men had assembled with excitement and expectation of experiencing the Lord in a fresh way. I knew that the Lord would not let them down.

One of the words the Holy Spirit spoke through me was that someone present had a skin condition on his back that God was removing. Later that night, a dear brother in his early seventies, who had been in the meeting, retired to his room. His roommate for the weekend happened to be a physician. When the older gentleman dressed for bed, the physician noted that the skin on the man's back was flawless and totally healed. This man's skin condition had been so bad, that for over twenty years his wife had nightly treated his back with an ointment.

But the story doesn't end there. This same man, fourteen years earlier had undergone surgery which destroyed his olfactory nerves. As a result, he had no sense of smell. He had smelled nothing for the past fourteen years.

However, the following morning (after the skin on his back was healed), he awoke early and smelled bread cooking. His sense of smell had also been healed! And the first thing he smelled was a pleasant aroma from the retreat kitchen where breakfast was being prepared.

God always does beyond what we ask or think!

Touching Limitless Power

The word of knowledge given that evening only described the man's skin condition on his back. Yet God even healed **beyond** what the Holy Spirit had articulated.

We haven't understood something about God. He **always** does exceedingly beyond what we ask and believe for.

It seems that once the Lord got His foot in the door and faith began arising in this man, His desire was to see what else He could do to bring glory to Himself. The miracle was perpetual. Faith was building. During the next meeting, the Lord spoke again. This time it was regarding the wife of one of the men. The Holy Spirit revealed that this man's wife had a lump on her breast. A phone call less than twenty-four hours later from the man's wife, confirmed that the lump had disappeared!

I believe God experiences a divine frustration. He always desires to do more than we let Him do, especially when saints gather together. God delights to express His glory with signs and wonders and prophetic manifestations, but men place great limitations on His Spirit.

Indeed the greatest hindrances to the word of God, and the moving of His Spirit, are the **traditions of men**.

> *'And He said to them, "All too well you reject the commandment of God, that you may keep your tradition."'*
> (Mark 7:9)

The second greatest hindrance to the flow of the Holy Spirit is **human respect**.

'For they loved the praise of men more than the praise of God.'

(John 12:43)

Men so often use such words as 'balance' and 'order' but the bottom line is, they are afraid to let the Spirit move as He wills.

Those who preach about balance the loudest, usually are saying it out of the desire to stay respectable, and the fear of what people will think. The lack of the Holy Spirit activity in their meetings depicts that by balance, they mean boredom. Balance is when God is totally in charge. And if He is in charge, awesome manifestations will be taking place. God desires that His Spirit move and miracles occur, and people are set free. **That's balance**.

There are no shortages of sermons regarding the subjects of the miraculous and the gifts of the Spirit. The problem is, most of it is just talk. We must stop talking about it and start doing it. And doing it may require sacrificing 'sermon time' so the Spirit has time to move.

My wife and I specifically inquired of the Lord why there is not more demonstration and manifestation of the super-natural in general in the church today. He said to us, 'The gifts of the Spirit are not an option, but many won't yield to them because men want safety zones and view them as too risky.'

Desperation

Desperation is the key to getting prayers answered. God always responds when we cry out in desperation to Him. The problem is that we don't stay desperate – desperate in our need for Him. When things are going smoothly, we get comfortable and cease to live with an intense need and demand of His presence in our lives.

The purpose of desperation is to provoke us unto God, that we might search out His limitlessness, desiring to experience more of Him.

Desperation leads to expectation. Expectation leads to miracles.

How easily we settle for the bondage of the mediocre, the mundane, and mere existence instead of the exhilaration of living. God calls us to be daring in our obedience, bold in our proclamation, and excitable in our expression of Him.

God has no concept of limitation. He doesn't think like we think. His thoughts are higher than ours. Consider God's perspective. He doesn't even see the impossible. How could He? He is God! Therefore, as we approach God, we must put aside all limitation and unbelief and meet Him on the grounds and language of faith. He is not limited by any thing or any person. All that limits Him is our own limitation of vision and our low level of expectation. That is why we have to be dauntless in our obedience and bold when we come before Him in prayer (see Hebrews 10:19).

Seems Too Good to be True

Since God's thoughts are higher than our thoughts, our minds cannot begin to conceive the plans God has for us. We can't understand it any more than a two-year-old child understands the trust fund his parents have set up for him. We have to have a simple childlike trust in God.

All limitation begins with the analytical mind. The more we scrutinize and try to figure God out, the more we establish walls of limitation in our own minds. That is where faith and trust come in. The natural reasoning mind was not created to understand spiritual things. Spiritual understanding comes by revelation of the Holy Spirit (see Ephesians 1:16–17).

In my final months of college I often prayed demanding that the Lord reveal His entire plan for my life. Looking back, even if He had told me, I know I wouldn't have believed it. It is always God's way to reveal His unfolding plan for our lives little by little, lest we **defile** what He has called us to do, by bringing it to pass in our own way (as Moses killed the Egyptian). Frankly, it is none of our business (and can easily ensnare us to become too preoccupied with the future) until the Lord is ready to reveal it to us.

Two years after graduation and working in the business

world, He instructed me to resign my position, and travel as a co-evangelist with a Catholic priest for the next three years. The circumstances that brought that event about were very miraculous. What seemed ridiculous was that during this same time I had been praying for a wife. Instead of answering my prayer, God provided me with an opportunity to travel with a Catholic priest. It sure proved to me that God has a sense of humor.

> *'For I will work a work in your days which you would not believe, though it were told you.'*
>
> (Habakkuk 1:5)

It is safe to say that God's plans are always **greater** than our own. He knows the end from the beginning. He knows the abilities and desires that He has given us, and His plan is that of perfection and fulfillment. Our problem is that we thwart these plans by our unbelief. All unbelief comes from analyzing. The more we analyze, the smaller God becomes in our own mind. It is like standing at the airport refusing to get on a plane until you understand how a one-hundred ton jet is going to get off the ground. The longer you think, the more impossible it seems to be.

Thinking Small

By far, the most common words I hear in reply, when I am encouraging someone to think bigger and to believe God in a greater way, are 'Yeah, but.' There is something about thinking small that is so snug and comfortable.

When someone has faced a disappointment in life, wherein some presumed plans didn't work out, I have found this truth applies, 'When God says "no" He has something better.' In other words, we must recognize that God has our best interest in mind. That is reality! We are a covenant people. Therefore, we should not be disappointed when God says 'no.' Rather, we can rest in His love and concern for us that He has something better in mind. He always does! Besides, He knows the end from the beginning. In fact, He **is** the end and the beginning, the Alpha and the Omega.

God is not limited by the plans our minds have conceived to work in our situation. Yet this is where we are threatened and so easily embrace discouragement. We usually are offended that the Lord has not 'blessed' the design we had worked out for the solution to our problem. Our man-made designs always limit God, for He will work in a way far beyond what our minds can conceive. He is God.

Plunging Into God's Limitless Arena

A wonderful example of the limitlessness of God was the situation when Jesus challenged Philip to believe beyond his limitation.

> *'Then Jesus lifted up His eyes, and seeing a great multitude coming toward Him, He said to Philip, "Where shall we buy bread, that these may eat?"'*
>
> (John 6:5)

> *'But this He said to test him, for He Himself knew what He would do.'*
>
> (vs. 6)

I love what Jesus did here. He confronted the ability of the natural, reasoning mind.

It didn't take Philip long to exhaust his resources. His mind could conceive little. He put a demand on his own mind (and resources) rather than on God.

> *'Philip answered Him, "Two hundred denarii worth of bread is not sufficient for them, that every one of them may have a little."'*
>
> (vs. 7)

But that is just the point Jesus wanted to make. As soon as we acknowledge the limitation of our minds, we are on the threshold of stepping into the miraculous, into the limitlessness of God.

The mind of man echoes with limitation. Philip was straining to understand how each one could have 'a little.'

That is how futile the arena of reasoning is; a little for me, a little for you, and very little for the pastor.

Philip did the best he could with his thinking capacity. Two hundred denarii worth of bread (a denarius was about a day's wage) would not even begin to feed this many people.

Then Andrew stepped forward to tell of a lad with five barley loaves and two small fish.

Jesus knew from the beginning that He was going to release an awesome miracle from the Father's hand. But He had this conversation with Philip in order to **expose the frustration** of trying to conceive miracles through the confines of our minds.

Jesus doesn't rebuke Philip, He just told the disciples to have the people sit down.

> *'Then Jesus said, "Make the people sit down." Now there was much grass in the place. So the men sat down, in number about five thousand.'*
>
> (vs. 10)

As Much as They Wanted

Our minds are enclosed with high walls of limitation, but the Spirit of God desires to pull those walls down. Most people have a mentality that if we reach into God for too much, we are somehow going to bankrupt His reservoir of abundance. It is time to let all limitation be removed from our vocabulary. The next verse is especially enlightening.

> *'And Jesus took the loaves, and when He had given thanks He distributed them to the disciples, and the disciples to those sitting down; and likewise of the fish, **as much as they wanted**.*
>
> (vs. 11)

This is always God's position. They could have as much as they wanted! We stop too short. We fail to press in with a posture of aggressiveness. We are picky eaters.

These are days when we must plunge into the limitlessness of God and dare to believe for the miraculous.

When we need a miracle, we must quickly acknowledge the limitation of our minds. Then we can take the plunge and dare to believe for the perpetual and endless flow that God has available.

The problem is not the devil. The problem has been our own perception of limitation.

Eat as much as you want!

Living in the Overflow

God is an 'exceedingly abundant' God. He promises to lavish upon us. *'That He lavished on us with all wisdom and understanding.'* (Ephesians 1:8 NIV) His promises all speak of abundance and generosity. God is generous in His grace, His forgiveness and mercy. Concerning our sins, He promises not only to pardon, but to abundantly pardon.

> *'Let the wicked forsake his way, and the unrighteous man his thoughts; let him return to the Lord, and He will have mercy upon him; and to our God, for He will **abundantly pardon**.'*

> (Isaiah 55:7)

In His mercy He is abundant and generous.

> *'The Lord is merciful and gracious, slow to anger and **abounding in mercy**.'*

> (Psalm 103:8)

> *'But You, O Lord, are a God **full of compassion**, and gracious, longsuffering and abundant in mercy and truth.'*

> (Psalm 86:15)

He is even generous as He blesses in prosperity. It is the very nature of God to be generous, and it is no problem for Him to bless, as long as our motives are not those of greed and selfishness.

The very nature of God is that He is more than enough and more than sufficient. He is called the 'All-sufficient One.'

I have found this 'overflow' principle to be true in a very personal and practical level. For example, in meetings where I've been invited to speak, the Lord will frequently give words of knowledge of miracles that He is bringing about. When a word comes forth that God is healing someone with a problem in his left knee, for instance, usually there are several people who are healed in their left knee during that meeting. One person may have been specifically praying for his knee, and putting a demand on the presence of the Lord. The Lord has heard and responded to that one person's fervency and desperation, yet when the Holy Spirit begins to move, several others are healed. Why?

They receive the overflow!

It is as if the power of God is so great and abundant that the residual power heals several others. It is similar to spraying one person with a water hose, but those within a few feet get wet too. Similarly, if a farmer prays hard for rain, and the Lord hears, the neighbor who may not have prayed, enjoys the benefits of the rain.

God works in the overflow principle. Faith takes hold in the same way. When a testimony is spoken how God healed one person, faith ignites in someone else, and soon the faith level is high, and numerous people are 'pulling' virtue out of God. God is glorified! That is why testimonies are important. Especially very recent ones. They build faith. And without faith, we cannot please God.

Remember the last miracle that God did through Elisha? Actually, this miracle completed the exact doubling to fulfill the double portion Elisha had requested from Elijah.

Elisha was dead and in his grave, but when a dead man was let down into Elisha's tomb, and touched the prophet's bones, he came back to life! Talk about overflow!

> *'So it was, as they were burying a man, that suddenly they spied a band of raiders; and they put the man in the tomb of Elisha; and when the man was let down and touched the bones of Elisha, he revived and stood on his feet.'*
>
> (2 Kings 13:20–21)

God wants us so dead to our selfish desires and motives,

that when those with great needs touch us, resurrection life flows into them.

You Cannot Bankrupt God

The mentality of much of the human race is that of deficits, shortages and scantness. Yet God speaks out of abundance in all creation. He even calls a scant measure cursed.

> *'And the short (scant) measure that is an abomination?'*
> (Micah 6:10)

The mentality of people when it comes to receiving from God is most always in limitation and scantness. Somehow we've derived this mental picture of God with a limited reservoir of goodness; a reservoir that has been extremely over-taxed with the pressing needs of humanity.

However, the Biblical picture is quite the opposite. *'The earth is the Lord's, and all its fullness.'* (Psalm 24:1) All that we need is available for us. The greatest problem God contends with are the limitations in our minds, which promote an unwillingness to press in to Him persistently for the miraculous.

Jesus exhorts us to **keep on** asking, seeking, and knocking.

> *'And I say to you, ask, (and keep on asking) and it will be given to you; seek, (and keep on seeking) and you will find; knock, (and keep on knocking) and it will be opened to you.'*
> (Luke 11:9 Amplified)

Why the Devil Hinders You and Me

The devil hates the expression of God through **any** person.

The devil hates noting more than to see the child of God walking in victory. Although he asserts no legal power over us, his strategy is to suppress the expression of God by coercing us to accept his thoughts of limitation, unbelief, and discouragement. That is the reason something simple, such as praising the Lord, can be difficult.

The devil has not changed style or methods. He attacks through the thought life. His strategy is to get us to accept his thoughts as our own! He doles out thoughts which quickly run through our minds. These diabolical thoughts come in a variety of forms; God's lack of concern for us, mocking thoughts, and thoughts of God's inability to bring about what we've believed Him for. Of course, the enemy will try to plant countless other seeds of discouragement and doubt to try to get unbelief to dominate our lives.

His aim is to endeavor to suppress you into keeping your thoughts limited and negative. He will try everything within his power to prevent you thinking and perceiving in the limitlessness of God. He's a liar, and we've been given authority over him.

> *'Behold, I give you the authority to trample on serpents and scorpions, and over all the power of the enemy, and nothing shall by any means hurt you.'*
>
> (Luke 10:19)

Depressing Thoughts

Depression is rooted in self-centeredness. If you don't think so, just think about yourself for fifteen minutes. You will feel yourself beginning to get depressed. God hasn't created us to dwell on ourselves. We were created to think on Him.

> *'Finally, brethren, whatever things are true, whatever things are noble, whatever things are just, whatever things are pure, whatever things are lovely, whatever things are of good report, if there is any virtue and if there is anything praiseworthy – meditate on these things.'*
>
> (Philippians 4:8)

Depression is probably the most used 'tool' of the enemy. When we open the door through self-centered thinking, the evil spirits stand in line to join the pity-party. Remember, **we** open the door. We are guilty of giving evil spirits the invitation. The devil will baby-sit any harboring of depressing thoughts or thoughts of self-pity. As one wise preacher rightly said, 'Self-pity is Satan's babysitter without charge.'

We must learn to hate depression! God hates it! No parent enjoys seeing his child depressed. Neither does our heavenly Father enjoy seeing us depressed or discouraged in any way.

We can quickly repent (make a decisive about-face action) of giving in to these thoughts and then command the devil to flee. He has no choice once we repent and submit ourselves to God.

> *'Therefore submit to God. Resist the devil and he will flee from you.'*
>
> (James 4:7)

The greatest truth about depression and discouragement is that discouraged people place **no demand** on the Spirit of God. No wonder the devil wants people discouraged! There is no faith or expectation in discouragement.

When we talk to Jesus, we are talking to the Creator of the universe. Begin to dwell on His greatness. Thank Him for all the things He's done in your life. Count your blessings!

Have you considered that the reason the devil comes against you in the first place is to suppress the thoughts and plans that God has for you?

> *'For I know the thoughts that I think toward you, says the Lord, thoughts of peace and not of evil, to give you a future and a hope. Then you will call upon Me and go and pray to Me, and I will listen to you. And you will seek Me and find Me, when you search for Me with all your heart.'*
>
> (Jeremiah 29:11–13)

Pressing Into God

There is something about the nature of God that is so easily overlooked. All things are available to us by calling on His name, but much tragically goes unclaimed, because people fail to press into Him.

Pressing into God involves not only prayer, but persistent prayer. Jesus instructed his disciples in His parable of the unrighteous judge, this principle of praying. The parable is prefaced by these words, *'Then He spoke a parable to them, that men always ought to **pray and not lose heart**.'* (Luke 18:1)

The first temptation as you or I begin to pray, is to lose heart. The situation overwhelms us, and the devil tells us that it is just too big, or too insignificant for God. But an attitude of intense expectation on our part is required by God. Half-hearted prayer requests seem to do little more than waste breath and time.

I often exhort people in a worship service where we are anticipating the move of the Spirit, 'If you can't get excited, act like it!' God is worth it! If we really are approaching God, why insult Him with lukewarm prayers, and half-hearted praises?

God is worth it. He is worthy of our praise and worship; but He is also worthy of our anticipation and expectation of His moving in our midst. Someone said, 'Blessed are they who expect nothing, for they will not be disappointed.'

Anytime we approach God, we should come with awe and expectation. Expectation places a demand on His presence.

God delights in the manifestation of His Spirit in the midst of His people. He is glorified when people are miraculously healed or delivered. He is glorified when numerous people testify of physical miracles they received as they entered into the presence of the Lord. Is He glorified by unbelief? Is He glorified when we go to a meeting with no expectation, exhibiting a 'business as usual' attitude?

I believe that any time the saints assemble, God desires to manifest Himself, and that we should always leave the meeting giving glory to His name for the great things He's done.

> *'Men shall speak of the might of Your awesome acts, and I will declare Your greatness.'*
>
> (Psalm 145:6)

Pulling Things Out of God

Another way to express the issue of pressing into God, is that of pulling things out of God. This is a heart-set and a mind-set that is pleasing to the Lord. The woman with the issue of blood (see Mark 5 and Luke 8) 'pulled' virtue out of Jesus when she moved in faith through the crowd, determined to touch His clothes. So strong was the pulling, that He turned around to say, *'Who touched me?'* She had expectation, not just a curiosity or interest.

My wife and I have ministered in numerous meetings where people have pulled things out of God. For example, someone will come to us after our meeting, having received a miracle, to tell us what happened. The person will explain how he put a demand on God for a specific need. Then, my wife or I spoke out the need in a word of knowledge during the meeting (having no foreknowledge of this person's need), and the person was healed. The exciting thing is that we realize that the Lord may not have given us the word of knowledge if that person had not put a demand on His presence. That person had the key. Expectation puts a demand on the limitlessness of God.

He has limitless resources at our disposal, but we must set our hearts to 'pull' it out of Him. If we don't, we will receive little.

It is always interesting when we pray for individuals. Some people are so hungry for God, that the minute we begin to pray their hunger 'pulls' virtue out of us. Oftentimes when hunger is present in them a prophetic word, or words of knowledge will come forth concerning the specifics of their situations.

However, when people are not hungry, the Spirit says little to them. The reason is simple. They are not exerting any demand on the presence of God. We stand amazed, because we are willing to speak the word of the Lord to them, but little comes because they are not in a mode of expectation.

The point is, we are the same people, the same willing instruments. But the amount the Lord uses us depends not on us, but upon the **level of expectation** of those present. Frankly, when someone is 'pulling' something out of God, and He uses us in their behalf, we can take no credit, as it is **their** hunger which is causing the Spirit to move in their behalf.

Emotion or Emotionalism

So many people say they are afraid of emotions. But that is not really true. What they are afraid of is emotionalism.

After all, if you received a letter in the mail telling you that you were the winner of a contest and would be awarded several thousand dollars, it would be difficult not to show emotion. In fact, even the most stoic and dispassionate person would be showing emotion.

Therefore, the issue is not over emotion, but emotionalism.

A wonderful analogy was shared a number of years ago by my friend, John Garlington. He explained it this way: you go to a football game and cheer and yell for two hours. In your enthusiasm you may also spill Coke and popcorn, and get quite obnoxious as you 'scold' the referee. That is emotion! And that is certainly viewed as normal.

However, emotionalism could be described as being in a football stadium, and cheering and yelling and knocking over Coke and popcorn, and 'scolding' the referee ... but there is no one on the field!

It is good to show emotion when God is doing something, but it is only emotionalism if you are just showing emotion and nothing is happening.

But whatever God is doing; it is worth getting emotional about.

Plunge into the limitlessness of God!

Chapter 4

The Spirit of Saul

– Externally, Saul was perfect. His stature, his looks, and no doubt his magnetic personality would make any mother proud. But internally, he was a man-pleasing, compromising, and distracted kind of guy –

> *'Now there was a long war between the house of Saul and the house of David. But David grew stronger and stronger, and the house of Saul grew weaker and weaker.'*
>
> (2 Samuel 3:1)

Early on, I couldn't put my finger on it. Various ones in leadership, left a deadness in my spirit. When they preached, it was canned and professionalized. There was a peculiar lack of humility and compassion. In conversations with them, I felt like I was being coerced on a deal to buy a used car that had a bad transmission.

Years later, I began to understand. I was seeing the spirit of Saul, and not that of David, a spirit that was fully dedicated to **know** the heart of God.

There are two natures of Christians – those who have the spirit of Saul, and those who have the spirit of David.

To follow Jesus Christ means to follow Him fully. It involves surrendering ourselves completely to His plan and purpose. To take up our cross and follow Him means to **deny** our own desires and endeavor to **obey** his Spirit with every fiber of our being.

Saul represents what human nature wants. He represents the will of man – man's way of fulfilling the purposes of God. David represents those who are desiring to please the Lord and to follow Him with all their heart. *'I have found David, the son of Jesse, a man after My own heart, who will do all My will.'* (Acts 13:22)

Carnal People Want Carnal Things

When Israel asked for a king, their main motive in desiring one was that all the other nations had kings. *'Now make us a king to judge us like all the nations.'* (1 Samuel 8:5)

The heart of God was grieved, as He, alone, desired to rule over them. Nonetheless, He gave them their wish.

> *'And the Lord said to Samuel, "Heed the voice of the people in all that they say to you; for they have not rejected you, but they have rejected Me, that I should not reign over them."'*
>
> (1 Samuel 8:7)

But their wish did not come without an ominous warning. Their king would **take** from them until they would cry out in vain from their bondage. Samuel warned them of the exact behavior their king would possess. He would **take** their sons to be his horsemen, to run with chariots, to plow his ground and reap his harvest, to make weapons of war and equipment for his chariots. He would **take** their daughters to be perfumers, cooks and bakers. He would **take** the best of their fields, vineyards, and olive groves for his own servants. He would put to work their best servants for his own work. He would **take** a tenth of their sheep. He would make them his servants (see 1 Samuel 8:11–22).

Yet, in spite of the warning, came the nauseous response of the people.

> *'Nevertheless the people refused to obey the voice of*

Samuel; and they said, "No, but we will have a king over us."'

(vs. 19)

Saul was a taker. He took and took and took from them as the Lord had warned them.

But God, in His wisdom, let them have what they wanted. The old adage states, 'Be careful what you pray for, you might get it.'

Man Wants Man to Rule Over Him

The tragedy of the people in wanting a king to rule over them, was that they were rejecting God, Himself, to rule over them.

If we reject intimacy with the Holy Spirit to direct us in our lives, there will always be a Saul to take the place of the Holy Spirit.

Frequently I see this in the body of Christ. Men would rather be ruled by men than by God! They complain about the lack of the freedom of the Holy Spirit that their pastor allows, but in their next breath, they talk about what a wonderful man he is.

There is more of a price to pay to walk by the Spirit. To the flesh, it seems easier to have a man whom you can see, to tell you what to do.

This seemingly is a shortcut from going to all the trouble to seek the Lord and to wait before Him for direction.

Of course, God has a divine order. He has placed in the church the five-fold ministry: the apostle, prophet, evangelist, pastor, and teacher, for the equipping of the saints (see Ephesians 4:11). They are gifts by the Lord to equip the saints in their walk, but **not** to live their lives for them.

No man, no matter what office God has placed Him in, should take God's place in your fellowship and intimacy with the Holy Spirit. The five-fold ministry is not given to rule over people, but to equip and edify the body of Christ.

The anointing of the Holy Spirit promises to abide and teach every believer the mind of God.

> *'But the anointing which you have received from Him abides in you, and you do not need that anyone should teach you; but as the same anointing teaches you concerning all things, and is true, and is not a lie, and just as it has taught you, you will abide in Him.'*
>
> (1 John 2:27)

Human nature recoils at dependency on God. It frustrates the flesh to have to listen to the quiet voice of the Holy Spirit on the inside of us. How tempting it is to find a Saul, and just follow him.

But the exciting adventure of the new covenant means that each believer will come into that awesome covenant relationship with God, Himself.

> *'None of them shall teach his neighbor, and none his brother, saying, "know the Lord," for **all shall know me**, from the least of them to the greatest of them.'*
>
> (Hebrews 8:11)

Famines and Dry Spells

The body of Christ has been in a time of spiritual famine. God has allowed us to experience a dryness and a lack of anointing in order to provoke us to desire with more intensity the very breath of the Holy Spirit in our lives. Those dry places become the turning point, where we cry out to God in desperation for Him; where we refuse to be satisfied with the man-made synthetic system of so-called Christianity.

> *'"Behold, the days are coming," says the Lord God, "That I will send a famine on the land, not a famine of bread, nor a thirst for water, but of hearing the words of the Lord."'*
>
> (Amos 8:11)

God desires to get our full attention. For too long we have settled into the comfortable posture of business as usual and have lost our zeal for God, Himself.

The famine God has allowed is not physical, but for 'Thus saith the Lord.' There is not a famine for preaching! There is an abundance of preaching, but there is a lack of anointed oracles from God.

God is waiting for us to return to **Him**. Again, we must desire His very presence far more than what He can do for us.

There is always the temptation to take the goodness of God for granted. Few people pursue God because they **want Him**, but usually because the drastic terms of their present crisis gives them no choice. It is the mercy of God that takes us into times of dryness, and even desperation, in order that we will cry out to Him for the fresh move of the Spirit in our lives.

There is a great separation going on within the body of Christ. The plumb line has gone down. We must, as individual Christians, make a decision whether we want to embrace the spirit of Saul or the Spirit of David.

Why Follow Saul?

Human nature desires that which will appeal to the senses, as well as that which will be acceptable to our friends. People usually follow a carnal leader because they are carnal themselves. Carnal people are impressed with carnal leaders who possess carnal strength and wisdom.

> *'And he had a son named Saul, a choice and handsome young man. There was not a more handsome person than he among the children of Israel. From his shoulders upward he was taller than any of the people.'*
>
> (1 Samuel 9:2)

Externally, Saul was perfect. His stature, his looks, and no doubt his magnetic personality, would make any mother proud. But internally, he was a man-pleasing, compromising, and distracted kind of guy.

Head and Shoulders Thinking

God's wisdom was to let the people of Israel get what they wanted. He chose for them a king who appealed to their natural and carnal wisdom. Saul appeared to have his act together in the natural. However, although he was head and shoulders above the others physically – spiritually (as is usually the case) he was a wimp. But we have a tendency not to look for the internal strength and spirituality, but to the external.

I like to call it the 'head and shoulders' mentality. May God deliver us from it. Samuel, the prophet, was instructed to anoint the man who was head and shoulders above the others.

> *'So they ran and brought him from there; and when he stood among the people, he was taller than any of the people from his shoulders upward.'*
>
> (1 Samuel 10:23)

Clearly this 'head and shoulders' leader was in the permissive will of God. Since the people wanted someone who appealed to the externals, God let them have Saul. But he was weak and spineless internally.

It is interesting how God talked to Samuel about Saul.

> *'So when Samuel saw Saul, the Lord said to him, "There he is, the man of whom I spoke to you. This one shall reign over My people."'*
>
> (1 Samuel 9:17)

Notice He simply said that He would reign over the people, not that he was chosen or was anointed.

Saulish and Soulish

I like to refer to soulish people as Saulish and vice versa.

It helps to recognize a Saul type of spirit, by aligning the word, 'Saul,' with 'soul.' The soulish nature of our being (our intellect, emotions, and natural abilities) is what a Saul-type person relies on.

A Christian, who has no brokenness before God, is still operating out of his soul, and not out of his spirit. He is not living by an ongoing dependence upon the Holy Spirit. His view of serving God is not according to dependence upon God, but, rather, attempting to do his best to please God through his natural faculties.

Hearing what God is saying to His inner man is not of particular concern to the soulish-Saulish person because he is quite comfortable with his own 'ability' to please God. But natural ability, no matter how wonderful it is, can **never** bring forth the Spirit of God.

No wonder God often uses the weak and foolish things of this world to confound the wise (see 1 Corinthians 1:27).

God chose David, a man after His own heart, to be the King over Israel. As David represents a man dependent upon God – quick to repent, and full of worship – so we must be in order to touch God's heart.

The Lord warned Samuel not to judge by appearance, but by the Spirit. Samuel's choice was Eliab, because he was judging by outward appearance.

> *'But the Lord said to Samuel, "Do not look at his appearance or at his physical stature, because I have refused him. For the Lord does not see as man sees; for man looks at the outward appearance, but the Lord looks at the heart."'*

(1 Samuel 16:7)

God always looks at the attitude and condition of the heart, while man often is impressed with the external condition. The carnal nature always is impressed with the 'head and shoulders' person. It is an interesting observation that Samuel, himself, had to be corrected by the Lord, to not judge by the outward view. You would think that his eyes would have been opened by now, having seen the character of Saul. None of us is exempt from judging by outward appearance. God, give us eyes to see from **Your** perspective!

Saul leadership is what seems right in man's eyes. God is letting us see it for what it is, that we might become as David – after the very heart of God.

The Characteristics of a Saul Spirit

1. A tendency to depend upon natural strength and ability. The Saul spirit has developed a dependence upon Himself, and has surrounded himself with equally 'competent' people. He has not surrendered himself to the dealings of the Holy Spirit, whereby he would have to acknowledge his total dependence upon God.

2. A lack of humility. A Saul leader is not a broken vessel. He is proud of his leadership skills, and knows how to fluctuate his voice at just the right time. Usually this involves false humility, but is so convincing that it deceives many. There is not true humility, but the Saul leader has learned how to say the right things at the right time. As a result, the Saul-man is highly praised by people and they speak with great respect for him, although he has earned the respect illegitimately.

3. A reliance upon methods. God will never let a method take the place of His Spirit. Many sincere leaders dutifully function in a method, totally in ignorance that God has long since removed His presence. Leaders have let a method that worked beautifully at one time, replace the Holy Spirit. The Lord, of course will not stand for it, and simply removes His presence from their midst.

4. A non-risk taker. To move in the Spirit of God is risk-taking. Stepping out in faith to obey the Holy Spirit has no written guarantees. To find security in methods is a common mistake. We all love the safety and security of the familiar. To depend on God in a given moment to give a fresh word or command, is way too risky for Sauls, so they quietly submit to the way of the flesh, and exchange what could have been an awesome experience with God, for the moldy and musty and commonplace.

5. Not willing to pay the price. There is a price to pay to be dependent upon the Lord. The price to pay is time and discipline. It takes time to seek the Lord and to wait in His presence. The Saul leader is too obligated to people to afford much time to wait upon God. He has compromised his soul to be a people-pleaser.

6. No desperation for God. A Saul leader doesn't think he

needs God totally. Sure, he would appreciate His help, but in general he has learned to function comfortably dependent upon his own personality, his own knowledge of handling people, his own communication skills, his own talent and, after all, he is a well-liked fellow.

7. *Puny prayer life.* Sauls don't pray much. Oh sure, they go through the motions, and they might even attend the weekly church prayer meeting. But this is mainly for appearance's sake. After all, there are so many things to do. But his view of prayer is just something that Christians do. It is not a necessity of life, without which, he is helpless. No, a Saul is not a man of prayer; he is a man of the people. He is not seeking the heartbeat of God; he is trying to be sensitive to the heartbeat of the people.

9. *Ego.* There is nothing in this world more repulsive than an inflated ego. Ego projects 'Look at me. Look what I have done.' It is the opposite of humility. There is a good acronym for ego: Easing ... God ... Out.

Only God has the power to lift up or bring down. If God has lifted someone up, why should that person have the 'big head'? He certainly can't take credit for it.

There is no room for ego at the cross. Our lives were crucified with Him. Ego always projects itself as better than someone else, and should have no lodging place in the servant of God. Personally, I hate conversing with an ego-stricken Saul who makes me feel like he is doing me a favor talking with me.

Also, Sauls never ask your opinion. They are too busy expressing theirs. Humility is lost in their self-elevating knowledge of their ministerial proficiency.

10. *Greed.* God will judge all forms of greed. Many don't start out succumbing to greed, but get drawn into it at a later time. Saul was certainly no exception to this. God had forewarned the people. Saul would take and take and take (see 1 Samuel 8:11–22). If greed is not crucified, its ugly head will be revealed, and usually at the expense of other people, bringing a reproach on the body of Christ. When Simon, the sorcerer, offered Peter money for the power of the Spirit, Peter rebuked him and said, *'Your money perish with*

you ...' (Acts 8:20). Thank God there was nothing in Peter that responded to greed.

11. No regard for the Holy Spirit. What the Holy Spirit wants is not a major concern to a Saul. He is primarily interested in what He wants and what will make him look good. When the Holy Spirit desires to manifest Himself specifically in the operation of the gifts, a Saul will become uncomfortable and try to maintain control of the meeting. Whether the Holy Spirit is quenched or squelched does not bother the conscience of a Saul, because he is more concerned that no one is offended, and that things are 'in order.' But how can we call it 'order,' if the Spirit is not doing anything?

12. A form of godliness, and an appearance of being spiritual. A Saul says and does a lot of things outwardly that look spiritual, but when you take a closer look, so much is planned and canned. In fact, a Saul is usually a charmer, a silver-tongue, who knows just what to say to make the ladies smile, and the men nod approval. Sadly, many cannot discern between anointing and mere personality. *'Having a form of godliness but denying its power. And from such people turn away.'* (2 Timothy 3:5)

13. A preference for palatable Christianity over the true freedom of the Spirit. A Saul leader doesn't want to offend anyone. Therefore, he endeavors to keep all things as palatable as possible. If visitors come into the church, he is very uncomfortable with any manifestations of the Holy Spirit because after all, he doesn't want to offend anyone. But if we don't offer people the moving of the Holy Spirit, what else do we have to offer them?

14. Loves crowds, but doesn't like people. You've seen it happen before. He speaks before a big crowd, and is all smiles.

But when he is appreciated by a mere 'lowly' individual, he doesn't have time for him. The one who had a need is quickly brushed aside, and in fact often rudely ignored. However, a Saul will be quick to make himself available to the influential and prominent. *'Be kindly affectionate to one another with brotherly love, in honor **giving preference** to one another.'* (Romans 12:10)

15. Lacks compassion. Men will be more accountable to God in this area than any other. God is in the need-meeting business. Compassion (which is the love of God flowing through us) must be the highest priority in our lives. A lack of compassion is a lack of the gospel. Jesus was always moved with compassion when He ministered to people. Compassion always preceded the manifestation of the miraculous.

16. Quick to give pat answers. He will resort to quick, uncompassionate prayers, rather than take time to hear what the Holy Spirit is saying to an individual with a specific need. Sauls only see ministry as an efficiently run business and don't have time to listen to the Holy Spirit.

However, there is nothing more exciting than hearing the fresh oracle of the Lord in a specific situation. *'Man shall not live by bread alone, but by every word that **proceeds** from the mouth of God.'* (Matthew 4:4)

Sauls are Being Replaced With Davids

Saul's downfall didn't catch God by surprise. The acid test is always given in the classroom of **full** obedience. Sauls are comfortable with a rational obedience, but not obedience which goes contrary to the analytical mind.

The exposure of Saul's real person came at a point where the obedience involved required refusing that which was palatable to human reasoning.

The command from the Lord through Samuel was ultra clear.

> *'Now go and attack Amalek, and utterly destroy all that they have, and do not spare them. But kill both man and woman, infant and nursing child, ox and sheep, camel and donkey.'*

(1 Samuel 15:3)

Clearly, Saul's true colors were revealed without question.

*'But Saul and the people **spared** Agag and the best of the*

> *sheep, the oxen, the fatlings, the lambs, and all that was good, and were unwilling to utterly destroy them. But everything despised and worthless, that they utterly destroyed.'*

(vs. 9)

The Sparing Mentality

Human rationalization is an affront to the Spirit of God. Although the command had been clear to destroy everything, Saul spared the things that were best in his eyes.

Sparing, instead of killing, was defiant disobedience and rebellion by Saul.

A Saul always spares instead of obeys. That is where the dividing line is revealed. What a temptation it is to rely on human reasoning.

Partial obedience is disobedience. There is a price to pay to do it God's way. The price is clear . . . **obey fully**.

Since Saul's heart was inclined to disobey such a clear command from the Lord, the Lord knew that he would never obey fully in his kingship, so He began to take him down.

> *'I greatly regret that I have set up Saul as king, for he has turned back from following Me, and has not performed My commandments.'*

(vs. 11)

Saul's disobedience did not catch God by surprise. Despite God's foreknowledge, He let the people have what they wanted. But now He was ready to raise up a man after His own heart.

A Saul-type will always have a sparing mentality. He will **spare** the truth, in order to not hurt people's feelings. He will **spare** declaring the oracle of God to the people, so that He won't upset his denominational headquarters. He is so conditioned to 'sparing' that God cannot **trust** him to lead the people.

Perhaps the most frightening reality is that people tend to become like their leader. If he spares and cuts corners in obedience, he is setting an example that those following him will imitate.

The bottom line is that a Saul-type declares himself an exception to the rule. After all, 'God understands,' He reasons. So he lives in compromise ... and the church he pastors continues to grow. People still like the 'head and shoulders' leader who is determined to offend no one. Although many are starving spiritually, and they have not heard an anointed sermon in years, they love their pastor.

Deception

Saul's heart was so people-conscious that he didn't even seem to know that he had disobeyed. When Samuel approaches him, he doesn't seem to have a clue that something is wrong.

He calls out to Samuel,

> *'Blessed are you of the Lord! I have performed the commandment of the Lord.'*
>
> (vs. 13)

But Samuel's rebuttal brings about the sobering truth.

> *'But Samuel said, "What then is this bleating of sheep in my ears, and the lowing of the oxen which I hear?"'*
>
> (vs. 14)

There is always **evidence** if we have disobeyed God! We can't fool God. God is looking for the fruit which comes through full obedience.

Smarter Than God?

The number one rule of obedience is declaring God smarter than yourself. Saul didn't have that revelation. Although God told him to destroy everything, he figured surely God must have misspoken. Why not save the good stuff and sacrifice it to the Lord? This humanistic attitude is exactly what cost Saul his throne and is the very reason why God must remove the Sauls from leadership positions and replace them with Davids (leaders who are after His heart).

They are Never Wrong

A fresh characteristic of a Saul spirit appears. When Samuel confronts his disobedience, he blames the people.

> *'And Saul said, "They have brought them from the Amalekites: for **the people** spared the best of the sheep and oxen, to sacrifice to the Lord your God; and the rest we have utterly destroyed."'*

(vs. 15)

There is nothing more beautiful than a leader who will stand before the people of God, humble himself, and declare he missed the will of the Lord. Sauls never do this, because they are too busy passing the buck. Besides, they know that they will lose the following of the people.

But nothing could be farther from the truth. People aren't stupid. They want to follow someone who is big enough to admit when he is wrong. What a secure feeling it is to follow a leader who will quickly admit when he has given poor leadership. There is safety in following such a one, because such humility will keep Him in God's path. Praise the Lord for a teachable spirit.

Saul Gets His Head Handed to Him

When Saul is blaming the people and is making his weak defense, Samuel (who had a belly full) demands him to be quiet.

> *'Then Samuel said to Saul, **"Be quiet!"** And I will tell you what the Lord said to me last night.'*

Saul hears the rebuke from the Lord through Samuel.

> *'When you were little in your own eyes, were you not*

head of the tribes of Israel? And did not the Lord anoint you king over Israel?'

(vs. 17)

*'Why then did you not **obey** the voice of the Lord? Why did you swoop down on the spoil, and do evil in the sight of the Lord?'*

Saul is still choosing to be deceived!

'And Saul said to Samuel, "But I have obeyed the voice of the Lord, and gone on the mission on which the Lord sent me, and brought back Agag king of Amalek; I have utterly destroyed the Amalekites."'

(vs. 20)

He **again** blames the people.

*'But **the people** took of the plunder, sheep and oxen, the best of the things which should have been utterly destroyed, to sacrifice to the Lord your God in Gilgal.'*

(vs. 21)

Even in the face of divine judgement, Saul tries to lie his way out of his predicament. His ego was too big to repent and face the truth.

Rebellion is as Witchcraft

A classic deception is thinking that we can sacrifice to the Lord on our **own terms**, and that it will somehow find a way to God's heart. This couldn't be farther from the truth.

*'Has the Lord as great delight in burnt offerings and sacrifices, as in **obeying the voice** of the Lord? Behold, to obey is better than sacrifice, and **to heed** than the fat of rams. For **rebellion** is as the sin of witchcraft, and **stubbornness** is as iniquity and idolatry. Because you have rejected the word of the Lord, He also has rejected you from being king.'*

(vs. 22–23)

This is the key issue. One we do not take with nearly enough seriousness. Saul rejected the word of the Lord. He **refused to obey the oracle of God** that came to Him.

How easily this can be applied to the modern day Sauls. Saul had acted on Scripture by being willing to sacrifice the 'best' things to the Lord. But even though sacrificing was Scriptural, it was putridly humanistic, because he defiantly and stubbornly rejected the **voice** of the Lord! He also interpreted Scripture to mean what he wanted it to.

In our day, the voice of the Lord (combined with Scriptural direction) becomes the issue. It is easy to look spiritual and to appear obedient – but are we listening to the inward voice of the Holy Spirit? Or are we just mouthing and going through the motions? God keeps score.

Sauls Are Too Competent

God is warning His church. Just like Saul, we have become competent in **our** abilities to carry out the duties of leadership. We no longer need the Holy Spirit, per se. We have become 'good' at what we do. We have replaced Spirit-led living with professionalism, and spiritual pride.

Yet there is a longing deep within our hearts to feel the freshness of the anointing of God flowing through us again. As we cry out to God in repentance, He will again fill our vacant hearts with the pre-eminence of His presence.

> *'Deep calls unto deep at the noise of Your waterfalls ...'*
>
> (Psalm 42:7)

Chapter 5

The Carnal Mind

– Classic carnality: I want to serve God ... my way –

'...The carnal mind is enmity against God.'

(Romans 8:7)

As the plane circled the city, my wife and I were enthralled with the excitement of getting to the conference where we would be speaking.

We felt honored to be guests of this gathering of prominent businessmen and prestigious Christian leaders. In fact, because of the significance of the meeting we flew in early so we could spend an extra day in intense prayer.

When the Friday night meeting was ready to begin, we got off the elevator and walked toward the large conference room in the elegant hotel.

We were seated among many distinguished guests and served an exquisite meal. Soon, the singing began and I knew that before long, I would be introduced to bring the evening message. Both my wife and I were excited, as we felt that the Lord had spoken to us some very specific and encouraging things for the people gathered.

As the spokesman for the meeting was making a few announcements, a well-known charismatic leader (who was not one of the guest speakers) whispered something in the spokesman's ear. I found out later, that he asked him if he could share something for a few moments. The spokesman consented by saying, 'Okay, but I cannot allow you any more than five minutes.' The celebrated leader said, 'I don't even need that long, I just want to say a few things.'

The spokesman meekly introduced the man, explaining that he wanted to greet the people. The man got up and began to talk and drop names of important people he knew, and went on and on, bragging, then dropping more names. Soon, he had talked over an hour, and had insinuated numerous times in his 'message' that he needed several million dollars for a Christian project he was doing for the Lord.

When the man finally sat down, it was just minutes before ten p.m. The businessmen that had flown in from around the country looked extremely tired, both from travelling, and from boredom.

My wife and I looked at each other, wondering what to do. The gracious spokesman tried to bring the people's attention back to the purpose of the meeting. We were totally willing to surrender the meeting, and to dismiss the people so they could get some rest. So we prayed for guidance. Immediately the Holy Spirit spoke to us to proceed with our planned ministry, but to be very brief.

When I was introduced and began to speak, I could feel the presence of the Lord settle in the room. I only preached for about fifteen minutes, but the anointing was so intense, that the people began to look alert. Joy was returning to their faces. Soon, I asked my wife to join me on the platform. As we spoke what the Lord was giving us, several people were healed instantly. Then prophetic words came to several, and some were so overwhelmed by God's presence, that they wept. All this occurred in a total of twenty-five minutes.

As the meeting was dismissed, people got up obviously refreshed and invigorated by the presence of the Lord.

We were encouraged to hear a number of weeks later that this popular charismatic leader (who, by the way, left the meeting when I stood up to speak) wrote a letter of apology to the spokesman of that meeting.

But we beheld the wisdom of God that night. The people

gathered saw the contrast of the carnal mind of man, and the purity of the presence of the Lord. It was obvious that they saw the contrast between the flesh of man, which profits nothing, and the Spirit of the Lord.

Resisting Carnality

By far, the most powerful enemy that the Christian has to battle is the carnal mind. The carnal mind is accustomed to being in command of our lives. Yet it is the greatest obstacle that will thwart the move of the Holy Spirit in the life of the believer.

A common misconception is that the carnal mind only operates in the sinner, one who does not yet know God. But a Christian who is not listening to the Holy Spirit, and depending on his reason and intellect and fleshly ideas, is carnal minded.

Paul wrote to Christians (not sinners) as he addressed the problem of the carnal mind.

> *'For to be carnally minded is death, but to be spiritually minded is life and peace. Because the carnal mind is enmity against God; for it is not subject to the law of God, nor indeed can be.'*

> (Romans 8:6–7)

Meathead or Revelation

The word, carnal, is the Greek word, 'sarx,' meaning meat. It is safe to say that when we refuse to pay attention to the Spirit, we are meat-minded, or meatheads! It may sound like an insulting term, but when Christians refuse to seek the mind of God and consult with His Spirit, that is exactly what we become – meatheads.

Acknowledged by many as the best prayer in the Bible, was Paul's prayer for the church at Ephesus,

> *'That the God of our Lord Jesus Christ, the Father of glory, may give to you the spirit of wisdom and revelation*

> *in the knowledge of Him, the eyes of your understanding being enlightened; that you may know what is the hope of His calling, what are the riches of the glory of His inheritance in the saints.'*
>
> (Ephesians 1:17–18)

This prayer is intercession that these saints will hear from God by having (in their own spirits) the spirit of wisdom and revelation in the knowledge of God. What a privilege this is that our **own** spirit can gain in revelation and understanding of God, Himself!

Without the spirit of revelation, we really are 'meatheads' because our reasoning is merely flesh and blood.

No wonder Jesus rejoiced at Peter's response when He asked him, *'But who do you say that I am?'* (Matthew 16:15) Peter's instantaneous response had nothing to do with his intellect, or from studying all night. He answered,

> *'You are the Christ, the Son of the living God.'*
>
> (vs. 16)

Jesus responded joyously because Peter (by revelation) finally got the point. A sure indication of maturity in the Christian walk is when you begin to have revelation in your own spirit by hearing from the Father.

> *'Blessed are you, Simon Bar-Jonah, for flesh and blood has not revealed this to you, but My Father who is in heaven.'*
>
> (Matthew 16:17)

Hostility

To depend on the natural senses and intellect, rather than listening and paying attention to the mind of the Spirit, is not just a poor choice, it is operating with an **enemy** of God!

The hardest member to subject to the Holy Spirit is this natural and reasoning mind.

> *'Because the carnal mind is enmity (hostility) against God ...'*
>
> (Romans 8:7)

The word, enmity, means hostile or viciously opposed. Quite simply, the mind of the Holy Spirit comes by revelation, and His mind is revealed no other way. The natural or carnal mind is simply a product of deduction and reasoning, which has nothing to do with the mind of the Spirit.

When men try to give 'input' to the things of God (their input being a product of fleshly reasoning), it is offensive to God. The carnal mind is severely in contrast to the Holy Spirit. It is hostility toward God.

I used to wonder why the carnal mind was referred to as hostile towards God. Then the Lord revealed to me the reason. The carnal mind becomes a **substitute** for the Holy Spirit. Rather than listen to the Spirit, men depend on the carnal mind and label it as being the mind of the Spirit. How grieved the Holy Spirit must be in church board meetings, where the mind of man becomes a flippant substitute for the Holy Spirit. It is a defiant posture against the Holy Spirit.

The Intellect Was Created to be a Servant

The intellect is a gift from God. But it was not meant to have the ability to give spiritual direction. It was not intended to take the place of the Holy Spirit. The intellect was created to be a servant! It does make a great servant, but when it is given any other role in our spiritual lives, it becomes a hindrance to the Holy Spirit.

A servant only does what he is told. Sometimes fervent Christians are accused of being anti-intellectual, because they do not want to argue and debate over issues. But this is not a valid allegation, because a devout Christian is merely desiring to seek the **mind of the Spirit** concerning an issue.

Most would agree that it is impossible to become a Christian without knowing Christ. I would then point out that it is impossible to be spiritual, without knowing the Holy Spirit.

When it comes to knowing the mind of the Holy Spirit in a

given situation, the intellect is helpless! When we seek the Lord for direction in situations, most of the time what the Holy Spirit directs us to do, is the exact opposite of what our natural minds would dictate to us. But the Spirit is always right, and He saves us so much time and trouble.

The Holy Spirit Said

It is astounding, when reading through the book of Acts, how many times you will see the wording 'The Holy Spirit said.' It is obvious that the key to such a mighty move, in the church and in the lives of the apostles, was letting the Holy Spirit be in charge and to give the commands.

> *'Then **the Spirit said** to Philip, "Go near and overtake this chariot."'*
>
> (Acts 8:29)

> *'While Peter thought about the vision, **the Spirit said** to him, "Behold, three men are seeking you. Arise therefore, go down and go with them, doubting nothing; for I have sent them."'*
>
> (Acts 10:19–20)

> *'For **it seemed good to the Holy Spirit**, and to us, to lay upon you no greater burden than these necessary things.'*
>
> (Acts 15:28)

> *'Now **the Lord spoke to Paul in the night by a vision**, "Do not be afraid, but speak, and do not keep silent; for I am with you, and no one will attack you to hurt you; for I have many people in this city."'*
>
> (Acts 18:9–10)

> *'Except that the **Holy Spirit testifies** in every city, saying that chains and tribulations await me.'*
>
> (Acts 20:23)

> *'Now when they had gone through Phrygia and the region of Galatia, they were **forbidden by the Holy Spirit** to preach the word in Asia.'*
>
> (Acts 16:6)

> '*And a vision appeared to Paul in the night.* A man of Macedonia stood and pleaded with him, saying, "Come over to Macedonia and help us." Now after he had seen the vision, immediately we sought to go to Macedonia, concluding that the Lord had called us to preach the gospel to them.'
>
> (Acts 16:9–10)

The Son of Man Has No Place to Lay His Head

A familiar scripture is often quoted concerning Jesus' statement to his disciples.

> '*Then a certain scribe came and said to Him, "Teacher, I will follow you wherever You go." And Jesus said to him, "Foxes have holes and the birds of the air have nests, but the Son of man has nowhere to lay His head."*'
>
> (Matthew 8:20)

Jesus was not saying there were no motels available for him.

A Scribe had just told him he would follow him wherever he would go. Jesus responded to the man by saying He had nowhere to lay His head.

Do you see it? People acknowledge that they want to follow Jesus, but He is the Head, looking for a body to rest on. Who is the body? We are! If we want to follow Him wherever He goes, we will have to submit to His being our Head. He cannot be a King without people wanting Him to rule over them. People cannot fully follow Jesus without letting Him put His head on their body.

If we refuse to listen to our Head, as a way of life, we remain carnal Christians, and continue to operate as the heathen. We may not be sinning, but we are denying the Son of God the desire to rest His Headship on our lives.

Defining the Carnal Mind

The carnal mind is strong, demanding, insensitive, insecure, impatient, obstinate and analytical. It doesn't matter how long you've been a Christian, the carnal mind has to be 'put under' subjection daily.

Let's face it, the human will does not submit easily to the will of God, even if it is a Christian or charismatic human will. In fact, as the Holy Spirit begins to make inroads into our lives, it won't be long before His will conflicts with our will.

Most Christians have no problem serving God those first few weeks. We've all done it. We pray, 'Lord, just have your way in my life.' And at the time we pray it, we really mean it. But on Monday morning, when our plans are violated, it is easy to forget our commitment and resist the Holy Spirit.

The crux of Christian growth and maturity is learning to submit the carnal mind to the Holy Spirit.

Resisting the Holy Spirit

It isn't just the sinners who resist the Holy Spirit. In fact, who would argue that sinners would resist Him. That's what sinners do – they sin. But the religious leaders are far more accountable to God for resisting the precious Holy Spirit. When Stephen stood up against the Synagogue of the Freedmen, and the Scribes and Pharisees who challenged the power working through His life, he rebuked them for resisting the Holy Spirit.

> *'You stiff-necked and uncircumcised in heart and ears! You always resist the Holy Spirit; as your fathers did, so do you. Which of the prophets did your fathers not persecute? And they killed those who foretold the coming of the Just One, of whom you now have become the betrayers and murderers.'*
>
> (Acts 7:51–52)

Many church leaders today are guilty of rejecting the Holy Spirit.

Being Baptized in the Holy Spirit Doesn't Mean the Carnal Mind Disappears!

How easy it would be that if once we accepted Christ and were baptized in the Holy Spirit, our carnal mindedness would just evaporate. No, it is a life-long process to learn to subject our well-intentioned intellect, to the mind of the Spirit.

Isaiah proclaimed prophetically the divine description of the thinking of God.

> *'For My thoughts are not your thoughts, nor are your ways My ways, says the Lord. For as the heavens are higher than the earth, so are My ways higher than your ways, and My thoughts than your thoughts.'*
>
> (Isaiah 55:8–9)

It is exciting to note, however, that even though God's thoughts and ways are higher, they are not unattainable!

God wants us to come up higher in His presence and learn to listen to His thoughts and instructions.

However, we must be willing to pay the price to take the time to seek the Lord. In fact, having the mind of the Spirit necessitates literally changing our lifestyle, so as to live with a total receptivity to the Holy Spirit.

The Soulish Realm

Many Christians are content to live in the soulish realm. The soul, is the Greek word 'psuche', which is that part of us that is made up of our emotions, and our intellect. Quite frankly, it is possible to be born-again and to have had the experience of the baptism in the Holy Spirit and yet live in the soulish realm.

The writer of Hebrews makes this distinction.

> *'For the word of God is living and powerful, and sharper than any two-edged sword, piercing even to the division of **soul and spirit**, and of joints and marrow, and is a discerner of the thoughts and intents of the heart.'*
>
> (Hebrews 4:12)

The living Word of God discerns and separates the soul from the spirit. If we allow the living word of God to judge and expose our thoughts and motives, He will cause us to become fruitful and effective. His guidance will help us to spend our energy solely on increasing the things of the kingdom of God.

If not, we will have to give an account to Him.

> *'And there is no creature hidden from His sight, but all things are naked and open to the eyes of Him to whom we must give account.'*

> (Hebrews 4:14)

It is Easy to Obey God When it Was Something You Were Going to do Anyway!

One day my wife asked the Lord this question, 'Why don't more leaders seek **You** for direction?'

The Lord answered her, 'The flesh is in control.'

The carnal mind is strong. Our flesh loves to be in charge of the work we are doing for God. I like to put it this way, 'It is easy to obey God when it is something you were going to do anyway.'

The most classic carnal attitude is, 'I want to serve God, **My way!**'

This carnal attitude has to go to the cross. Selfish ambition is as witchcraft in the eyes of God.

> *'Who is wise and understanding among you? Let him show by good conduct that his works are done in the meekness of wisdom. But if you have bitter envy and self-seeking in your hearts, do not boast and lie against the truth. This wisdom does not descend from above, but is earthly, sensual, demonic.'*

> (James 3:13–16)

There is no question that God is dealing with this carnal attitude in the church. We must let Him purify our motives and cleanse us from all self-elevating ambitions. If we do not, we will never see His glory revealed.

The Holy Spirit Moves On

The Bible says in Genesis 6:3 *'My Spirit shall not strive with man forever ...'*

We must realize that, although the Spirit of God will woo us to go His way, if we continually ignore Him, He may eventually move on. His moving on may not necessarily keep us out of heaven, but it will certainly keep us from maturity and prevent His glory being revealed in us.

In the charismatic outpouring of the seventies, so many denominational people were baptized in the Holy Spirit. They not only received the initial evidence of speaking in tongues, but many had mind-boggling testimonies of the activity of the Holy Spirit in their lives.

Yet, tragically, many have departed from this visitation from God. Just as the hearts of the children of Israel were inclined to turn back to Egypt on their first momentary encounters with hunger and thirst, many have fled back to the warm womb of their denomination. They forgot the miracle of the Lord's visitation, and baptism in the power of the Holy Spirit.

During the late sixties and seventies, the sovereign move of the Holy Spirit was labeled as the 'Charismatic Movement.' Thousands from every denomination and every conceivable walk of life were filled with the Holy Spirit with the evidence of speaking in tongues.

Yet this experience was only meant to be a beginning or a threshold, certainly not the ultimate. The realm of the Holy Spirit brings us into a new intimacy with God and His power in the gifts of the Holy Spirit.

God never intended the Holy Spirit to make us stronger within our various denominational walls. He desired that we follow on with Him!

Hosea exhorted the believers with the same call the Holy Spirit gives today,

> *'Let us know, let us pursue the knowledge of the Lord ...'*

(Hosea 6:3)

Comfort Zones

There is no more pertinent message than to follow on with God.

It is always the will and desire of God to take us farther than we want to go.

Yet this is where human nature resists the hardest. We are continually searching for resting places and for comfortable and secure surroundings.

God, of course, wants us to be comfortable, only not just in our surroundings and circumstances, but in Him! There is no peace on the outside, until we let Him rule as with peace on the inside. When peace rules on the inside, then it will rule on the outside, over every situation.

Our humanness resists change, but if anything in life is certain, it is change.

I love to read in the Bible the few verses attributed to a man named Enoch. In Genesis we read,

> *'And Enoch walked with God; and he was not, for God took him.'*

(Genesis 5:24)

I've always pictured it this way. Daily Enoch and God are walking along in fellowship. Daily God reveals Himself to Enoch, and as He does, Enoch willingly yields up his habit or weakness, and lets the glory of God consume that area. Then one day, God looks at Enoch, and sees nothing in Enoch that has not surrendered to the Lord. At that point, God says to Enoch, 'We've walked so far that it is closer now to my house. Instead of going back to your house, let's just walk on to Mine.'

Enoch walked so intimately with God, that He disappeared! He let the Lord consume all His motives and desires until Enoch was no more. God honored him, by taking Him home without seeing death.

The will of God for each of us is that we disappear! Walking with God, and not resisting when He requires change will cause us to be consumed with His presence.

It is such a delight to be around saints who have let God

deal with them. There is no defensiveness, paranoia, and no evidence of a critical spirit. They don't talk about their church and how wonderful it is. They talk about God, and what fresh things He has been breathing and speaking into their lives.

Emotions are Foolers

When it comes to listening to God, the greatest temptation by far is to substitute the emotions for the voice of God. Your own emotions can convince you that you have heard the Lord.

For example, when someone comes up with an idea regarding a specific plan of action, the emotions usually embrace it quickly. Then as more input is given, the fleshly emotions get more and more excited, and soon you are convinced you have heard the Lord.

While pastoring a church in Texas, a piece of property came up for sale next door to our church. I was convinced that we needed to purchase the property for additional parking. The more my emotions got involved in it, the more excited I became. The price was reasonable, the need was there, and frankly it wasn't hard to convince the men on the board that this indeed was a plan of action we needed to take. A few weeks later, however, right before the final papers were signed, the Lord spoke to me in a dream, regarding the property. In brief, He was not in the plan. In obedience to the Lord, I had to repent to all the people I had gotten involved with, and back out of the deal. Soon thereafter, the Lord worked out a situation where we were allotted additional parking space at no cost to us.

I had no choice but to repent and admit that the entire plan was not born of the Spirit, but purely out of my emotional zeal. I tried to convince God what a good deal the property was, but obviously He wasn't impressed.

Preachers and the Carnal Mind

I am not speaking with a critical heart when I say that a large percentage of preachers function in their ministry out of their carnal minds. I believe it is just a fact.

The main reason for this is they are often distracted and almost always too busy. Secondly, they are not willing to pay the price to have their own agenda crucified.

When a pastor invites an evangelist to his church, oftentimes the invitation is extended out of emotions or carnal thinking rather than having been initiated by the Spirit of God. Often the Holy Spirit has not even been consulted in such matters.

Who is the head of the Church, we or Jesus? Whatever the Holy Spirit has not initiated is man-made.

The same thing is true with evangelists. There often is not a concern whether God is telling them to go to a certain church in a certain city. Many go without any release from the Spirit (and oftentimes with no effort exerted to seek God) anywhere they can get their foot in the door.

It makes one wonder what the motive of certain ministries is. Is it to obey God or to fill up their calendar?

We must let the Lord be the Head of the church again. This encompasses submitting our own heads to His headship.

When God Says 'No,' He Has Something Better

I have always prayed about decisions. In our marriage, my wife and I pray about everything. We enjoy seeking the Lord about speaking engagements, what subjects to minister on and write about, as well as personal decisions.

But my experience is this. Many of our ideas with which we excitedly approach the Holy Spirit, prove to just be ideas. In fact, when I seek the Lord about some idea I've had for a sermon, a place I am to preach, or even something I am going to buy, I am frequently told by the Holy Spirit, that it is not His wisdom.

Needless to say, this is hard on the flesh. My flesh (and yours too) wants God to bless our ideas and initiatives.

The good news is, that when He tells me an idea is not of Him, it is because He has something better. Without fail, if I am willing to lay down a desire to carry out one of my ministry ideas, or even a personal purchase that I desired to make, later something better will come along. The Holy Spirit will see to that! He is a trouble-saver, time saver, money-saver, and problem solver, to name a few.

But a lot of people choose to go the carnal route. Waiting on God frustrates them. They will even make light about people who wait on the Lord. But the lack of the Holy Spirit's breath and freshness in their lives, proves they are the ones who are missing out.

Taming the Emotions

Emotions are part of the soul. Only the living Word of God can separate the soul from the Spirit (Hebrews 4:12).

The best way to quiet the emotions, when it is difficult to distinguish whether you are hearing God or the emotions, is to rest in God. If it is at all possible, let the idea be put on the shelf for a few days. If it is of the flesh, your interest in it will die, for emotions don't give life, they fluctuate with your feelings. But if it is of God, it will not fade away, but the Holy Spirit excitement will remain.

We must exhibit a willingness to submit the strength and intensity of our emotions to the Holy Spirit. There is a price to pay. Enthused emotions can be so persuasive that you will be unequivocally convinced that you have heard from God. But the Holy Spirit can reveal the difference.

Prophets and the Carnal Mind

I have observed many prophetic ministries over the years. My observations are used to help me learn, not so I can make judgements. One thing I have concluded is that when people are in the Spirit, they are really in the Spirit, and when they are not in the Spirit, they are most assuredly not in the Spirit.

Let me emphasize this point again. Being used of God at one point doesn't guarantee that person will automatically be in tune to the Spirit at other times.

Actually, it is easy to be in the Spirit, when you are in the atmosphere of the Spirit. For example, if a person with a prophetic ministry is in a meeting, he may be so in tune with the Spirit that he may prophesy the oracle of the Lord with amazing accuracy.

But again, that does not guarantee that the same person will be in the Spirit on the next occasion. That individual has to make a continual choice to open himself up to the mind of the Spirit.

This is where people get confused. They figure that if someone has a prophetic ministry, he is somehow 'connected' in some special way to God at all times. Not necessarily! He must **continually** make himself open to the Spirit.

This is a warning to all Christians, namely to keep your eyes on the Lord. The same person who prophesied the word of the Lord to you and gave you life changing direction, may also be capable of giving you his opinion on another occasion. Never look to the vessel God uses. Appreciate the vessel, but look to God, and wait on the Holy Spirit to bear witness, no matter who is ministering.

No one is exempt from carnality. Frankly, any vessel that God has used, is capable of slipping out of the Spirit, and yielding to his own carnal mind. This can be a well-intentioned carnal mind, but it is still the carnal mind.

Thank God that the Holy Spirit within you will never deceive you and will guide you into all truth.

What has amazed me, as I have known many prophets personally, is this. When they are ministering in a church meeting, they are so **in tune** to the Lord. But these same prophets seem to miss God when they make major personal purchases, or accept speaking engagements (which God is not telling them to accept). I've seen many of them get into awkward situations, simply because they did not listen to the Spirit of the Lord.

It seems they don't understand that the same Holy Spirit, who flowed through them as they ministered to the people of God, will also flow through them on direction for their personal lives.

Somehow, we live under a false concept, that the anointing is present in meetings, but He is not nearly as available when we need specific direction in our lives. This is absurd.

He abides! We have to choose to listen to that inner voice of the Holy Spirit. Nothing on earth is more exciting or fulfilling than hearing the voice of the Lord.

Time Alone With God Kills Soulish Impulses

The Lord spoke to me one day the sentence: 'Time alone with Me will kill your soulish impulses.'

The best medicine for the carnal mind is to spend more time fellowshipping with God.

It takes **time** to know and understand the mind of the Holy Spirit.

The Bible says, *'But the people who **know** their God shall be strong, and carry out great exploits.'* (Daniel 11:32b)

Knowing God should be the highest desire of every Christian. It is out of our relationship with Him, that all things fall into proper perspective and order. When we don't take time to cultivate our love relationship with Him, we automatically begin relying on the soulish nature, and ignore impulses from the Spirit. The life in the Spirit is a life of listening. All our actions and decisions should revolve around 'tuning in' to the mind of the Spirit. The more we mature, our confidence in God increases, but confidence in our flesh diminishes.

> *'For we are the circumcision, who worship in the Spirit, rejoice in Christ Jesus, and have **no confidence** in the flesh.'*
>
> (Philippians 3:3)

What is Flesh?

What is flesh, anyway? Flesh is not just that which is hanging on our bones. We are flesh. It is the impulsion that comes out of our own desires – not the desires of God.

The best definition of flesh that I ever heard, was given by Pastor A.J. Rowden's wife, the late Margaret Rowden of Kansas City, Missouri. She wisely said, **'Flesh is anything that is not energized by the Holy Spirit.'**

God has created us to live by listening to the Holy Spirit. The desires of our flesh are always in contrast to the Spirit.

However, the more we mature in our walk with God, the more we become in tune to what the Spirit is saying to us. Also it becomes more obvious to discern fleshly impulses from the Spirit speaking to us. Becoming sensitive to God is a process. Moving presumptuously in the flesh (which we've all done), can become a learning experience if we take responsibility for our actions.

The Carnal Mind, the 'Last' Enemy to be Destroyed

It is interesting to note that Jesus was crucified at Golgotha. The word, Golgotha, means the place of the skull.

It is at the place of our skull, where we all must be crucified.

The carnal mind is that seemingly final enemy that must submit to the cross. Although we have obtained victory over sin through the blood of Jesus, we must also have victory in submitting our carnal thinking, and surrendering to the Lordship of Jesus Christ.

Although we are sinless, and have understood the grace of God in that we don't have to yield the members of our bodies to sin, we cannot let our own carnality substitute for the mind of the Spirit. Plainly, a forgiven and sinless life, can still be a life of carnality.

A pertinent example of carnal thinking was a situation that Paul addressed to the Corinthian church.

> *'For you are still carnal. For where there are envy, strife, and divisions among you, are you not **carnal and behaving like mere men?** For when one says, "I am of Paul," and another, "I am of Apollos," are ye not carnal?'*
>
> (1 Corinthians 3:3–4)

These were saved people, yet they were still thinking in status quo terms, just like the world. They still had a need to become spiritual. The only way to be spiritual is to think like God thinks. Only the Holy Spirit can communicate to you His thoughts.

Baby Christians Come in Adult Bodies

It is sad that many churches function in a carnal vein. They are run like a business, not like our Father's house.

So frequently, leaders are chosen, not by their spirituality, but by their business ability or financial stature. Shamefully, whether or not the man hears from God, or is a man of prayer, is hardly taken into consideration.

Sadly, this is true of many men's and women's Christian organizations. Quite often, brand new Christians are put in authority; so new in the Lord, they have not the faintest idea of how to let the Spirit lead them, any more than a new baby can drive a car. Yet carnal people judge by the exterior, and put babes in leadership.

As a pastor, I had to face the sobering truth. The problem with baby Christians is that they come in adult bodies!

I have seen many pastors go through needless and painful experiences, by putting people in leadership who were not mature enough for the position.

Most often the mistake is made of judging by external appearance. The pastor will pick someone to serve in a place of leadership who is respectable outwardly. Usually it will be a good business man or 'stable' family man. However, spiritually (in God's eyes) he is still in training pants. The pastor has made a carnal choice. Instead of praying and waiting on God, he has judged by outward appearances.

No leader should be designated or confirmed by man to be a leader until the Holy Spirit has confirmed that he is indeed called by God to be in that position.

Many divisions in church bodies are brought on by men who were prematurely put in authority by other men, and not by God. Then when the Spirit begins to direct things in a certain way, these spiritually immature men or women in authority do not understand the workings of the Spirit, and end up opposing the pastor. Of course, it is often the pastor's fault for elevating them to that position in the first place.

This is not to say pastors are themselves exempt from carnal mindedness. But the most pertinent qualities anyone in a position of leadership can possess is first of all, his appointment to that position by God, Himself. Secondly, he must possess the spiritual ability to discern and recognize God's voice, thus being able to move and flow with the direction of the Holy Spirit.

Knowing the Mind of the Spirit

Churches need to return to being a house of prayer, and not a house of sermons, or a house of religious organization, where we come to have our ears tickled and our ego stroked.

More than anything else, we must desire to come to know and understand the mind of the Spirit. All else is vanity.

> *'For "Who has known the mind of the Lord, that he may instruct Him?" But we have the mind of Christ.'*
> (1 Corinthians 2:16)

God even had to correct the prophet Samuel on this when it was time to anoint David. *'For the Lord does not see as man sees; for **man looks at the outward appearance, but the Lord looks at the heart**.'* (1 Samuel 16:7)

The baptism in the Holy Spirit doesn't guarantee maturity. What does guarantee maturity is when an individual lets the Holy Spirit deal with Him, and is willing to be broken by the Spirit. Broken vessels will not quickly be swayed or deceived by winds of adversity. Over time, the dealings of God have tempered them.

> *'That we should no longer be children, tossed to and fro and carried about with **every wind of doctrine, by the trickery of men**, in the cunning craftiness of deceitful plotting.'*
> (Ephesians 4:14)

We must have the mind of the Spirit. The Spirit sees beyond the external. He also has a good track record.

Chapter 6

Tormented People

– Depressed and tormented people suffer from a lack of vision –

> *'There is no fear in love; but perfect love casts out fear, because fear involves torment . . .'*
>
> (1 John 4:18)

The longer I live, I recognize more and more that the devil's strategy is to discourage, distract and destroy human beings through their thought life. Jesus addressed this dilemma by declaring and labeling the devil with only one ability and strategy. *'. . . for he is a liar and the father of lies.'* (John 8:44)

Then Jesus neutralized the thrust of the enemy by recapitulating his blueprint for all of mankind.

> *'The thief does not come except to steal and to kill, and to destroy. I have come that they may have life, and that they might have it more abundantly.'*
>
> (John 10:10)

Settle It!

God wants you to have abundant life! This is the issue that must be settled. Until it is settled within your individual heart, and that knowledge drenches your being, you will be

91

prey for the enemy's lies to accept defeat in various weak areas in your life.

This is not to say that there is some kind of Christian utopia and that a 'real' believer should never have problems. But with the Word of God as his weapon, the believer should always have victory. A believer goes through problems, trials and hindrances, but ends up on top. *'But thanks be to God! He gives us the victory through the Lord Jesus Christ.'* (1 Corinthians 15:57)

Defeat Always Begins in the Thought Life

It is in our thoughts where the enemy seeks to steal the victory.

> *'Casting down arguments (speculations) and every high (lofty) thing that exalts itself against the knowledge of God, bringing every thought into captivity to the obedience of Christ.'*
>
> (2 Corinthians 10:5)

Speculative thoughts of the enemy attempt to challenge the knowledge of God regarding your life. What is the knowledge of God? God has good plans for you! He desires you to live in health! He has blotted out your sin and you are a new creation who is led by His Spirit.

The enemy uses the ancient art of planting seeds of doubt by sowing speculative questions in your thoughts. 'What if this pain is cancer?' 'What if my business folds up?' 'What if I can't pay my bills?' I refer to these types of thoughts as the 'What ifs?' Often, the moment you begin to move toward God, the enemy will start with the 'What ifs?'

These speculative and imaginative thoughts are the devil's food. They attempt to dismiss the faithfulness of God and His steadfast love. But God has given you and me the authority to cast down and resist those thoughts, by actively bringing them captive to the Holy Spirit. These thoughts must be resisted and cast down! The believer must take an active and aggressive posture to resist **all** speculative thoughts.

*'Be sober, be vigilant; because your adversary the devil walks about like a roaring lion, seeking whom he may devour. **Resist him**, steadfast in the faith, knowing that the same sufferings are experienced by your brotherhood in the world.'*

(1 Peter 5:8–9)

Don't Entertain Those Thoughts

There is something about human nature that finds it easier to dwell on the negative than the positive. Because of this, we often find ourselves **entertaining** thoughts rather than **resisting** them. However, if we take a minute to entertain a speculative thought, the enemy quickly adds another one. And guess what? You begin to feel depressed and feel your victory slipping away.

Therefore, all negative, speculative and questioning thoughts must be challenged by the Word of God and resisted. The devil is an inchworm. He tries through the thought life to inch his way into your thinking. Don't accept his thoughts. Don't engage in a conversation with the devil. Entertaining one thought is nothing more than opening a door to many more. You can't stop the devil from hurling negative or discouraging thoughts, but you **can** refuse to entertain them.

You Need a Smaller Devil!

Many Christians depict a small God and a big devil. My advice is to trade in your 'big' devil for a smaller one. Some possess a 'big' personal devil because they let their 'devil' shoulder all the blame for their mistakes. If you must have a devil in your conversation, let it be a small one, who has been reduced only to a professional liar.

In the prophetic words of Isaiah, men at the end of time were looking down into a pit at the fallen Lucifer.

'Those who see you will gaze at you, and consider you, saying: "Is this the man who made the earth tremble, who

> *shook kingdoms, who made the world as a wilderness and destroyed its cities, who did not open the house of his prisoners?"'*

(Isaiah 14:16–17)

It grieves me to hear certain preachers dwell more on the power of the devil than on the awesome power of God. It leads me to believe if there were no devil, they would have nothing to preach about.

Books on the devil, especially with a scene of evil on the front cover, sell faster than any other Christian books. People seem to prefer the sensation of reading characteristics of the devil more than about the exalted Christ.

We need to exalt the Lord. And a wonderful way to exalt Him is to let Him rule our thought life; when every thought against our mind has been taken captive by the obedience of Christ.

Typical Depression Comes From Lack of Vision

I learned through my own son that depression often comes from a lack of vision. I would observe him being downcast at times, and then enjoying life to the fullest at other times. My wife and I saw a pattern developing. When he had something to look forward to, such as an activity after school, something specific going on in the coming weekend, or a minor compulsion with a new hobby, he would not give in to depression or melancholy.

However, on the days when life was routine, just going to a typical day of school, nothing special to do but live in America, in a nice home, with good food, and nice parents, he would start slipping into a melancholy state. Seeing his vinegar-dipped face, I would ask him what was wrong. Usually his answer was 'Nothing.' But when I would press him further to insist that he not entertain the devil's depression, he would usually blurt out, 'There's nothing to do!'

By the Spirit, we perceived that he was actually saying that there was nothing to look forward to. He was finding it impossible to function without a vision.

We quickly learned that he was the type of child who needed to be challenged. Rather than only rebuke the oppressive spirits that were seeking to sit on his shoulder until something more exciting happened, we also helped him to create something to do, something to look forward to.

Most Christians suffer from a lack of vision. That is why they often find themselves bored and depressed. Without a vision, life gets mundane too easily. Going to work. Coming home. Eating. Sleeping. God has built us in such a way that we need a vision in order to function to our full capacity and potential.

Many escape from a need for a vision by becoming workaholics or have countless outside stimuli that destroy their bodies or paralyze their souls. People who can't recognize their need for vision, often try to create excitement by extremes or exaggerations in behavior, chronic worrying, or wasteful habits.

God has created us to function by vision. Our lives have a purpose.

Depression Stifles Creativity

God is a creator. We have been created in His image and likeness (Genesis 1:26). Therefore, we are also creative.

The enemy would desire to destroy the God-given creativeness in each of us.

The enemy's onslaughts against the believer come in three general areas.

1. Confidence. It is in confidence that our creativity begins to flourish. Confident people are a joy to be around. Everyone gravitates to the confident. A significant poll of men and women several years ago, reported by Reader's Digest, showed conclusively that the attribute admired most in the opposite sex was that of confidence.

The devil desires to suppress the creative flow and potential of your God-given creativeness. Therefore, his strategy is to discourage. When discouragement sets its lethal claws in your mind, your confidence begins to evaporate, and all creativity stops. So much potential is thwarted by that all-to-familiar word, discouragement.

2. Joy. There is a truth that is as certain as the law of gravity. The joy of the Lord is your strength (Nehemiah 8:10).

The devil is the joy-robber. In fact the first thing he'll try to squelch is your joy. Joy and strength seem to operate on equal levels. Once your joy evaporates, your strength seems to follow. The quickest way to lose your joy (and the devil knows it) is to let all your thoughts dwell on yourself. Prolonged thoughts directed inward, will nearly guarantee depression and there will be no joy to be found. The old clever acronym was accurate. J-O-Y Jesus first. Others second. You ... last.

3. Vision. The devil doesn't attack your faith. He doesn't need to! He attacks your vision. Your faith is not your problem, your lack of vision is your problem! Like joy and strength, vision and faith go together. Your vision will tell your faith what to do. Faith will always cooperate and rise to the level of your vision. The greatest need among individual Christians is the need for vision. Churches are full of visionless people. Spiritually, their vision often doesn't go farther than just going to church. This is tragic, since God has created each of us with unlimited potential. Don't leave it up to the pastor of your spiritual mentor. Seek God!

Pray for Vision, and Depression Will Leave

Vision is the divine escape from boredom and depression. Pray for vision daily. Make it your prioritized prayer. Everything else in your life will gravitate toward the vision of God's plan and purpose for you. Even though you don't see a change all at once, keep praying! God will unveil His vision for you, even if it is a little at a time. Be obedient to what He shows you.

> *'He who is faithful in what is least is faithful also in much, and he who is unjust in what is least is unjust also in much.'*
>
> (Luke 16:10)

What a truth! Don't be fooled by the sensational. God

often directs us to take steps. Each step, although small, guarantees you are moving.

'For who has despised the day of small things?'
(Zechariah 4:10)

Depressed People see in Distortion

I'll never forget the morning the Holy Spirit spoke to my wife these words, 'Depressed people see and hear in distortion.' Through the mind of the depressed, everything is negative. Like a person with good eyesight trying on prescription glasses, the whole world has become distorted. Or when a small child has gone too long without a nap, he fusses at everything, and there is nothing that can please him. His whole world is distorted until he gets his nap.

That is why we cannot 'give in' to depression for even a moment. Depression is the devil's gospel. It is his attempt to cut you off from the ongoing goodness of God.

Jesus had eyes to see what the Father was doing.

'... the Son can do nothing of Himself, but what He sees the Father do; for whatever He does, the Son also does in like manner.'
(John 5:19)

Likewise we need eyes to see what the Father is doing in our individual lives. How can anyone be depressed who has a vision of what the Father is doing in his life?

A great deal of the preaching of the gospel in years past has been beating the sheep instead of feeding the sheep. Guilt makes people run from God, which is the very means through which some preachers attempt to motivate people. But instead of always leaving a church service with the familiar, 'You're not doing enough for God' syndrome, we should leave with a fresh challenge and renewed hope and desire to recognize what the Lord **is** performing in our particular lives.

The Problem of Self-Centeredness

All self-centeredness is potential mental illness. Those who never mature beyond this inward-glaring state will only progress to further depths of anguish. God has made us to be more conscious of Him and the needs of others more than ourselves.

> *'We then who are strong ought to bear with the scruples of the weak, **and not to please ourselves**. Let each of us please his neighbor for his good, leading to edification. For even Christ did not please Himself; but as it is written, "The reproaches of those who reproached You fell on Me."'*

(Romans 15:1–3)

It disturbs me to talk to a Christian in a lengthy conversation and to listen to him talk about himself, his job, his ministry, his children, his problems, and never once ask me how I am dong. I often secretly use this as a measuring stick to recognize how embedded that person is in self-centeredness.

It is not unusual, even among ministers, never to hear a question about your own needs. It is discourteous, not to mention un-Christlike.

One minister in particular, as I have conversed with him over the years, has never once asked me about my family or children. Every time I talk to him, I am always careful to ask him about his wife and each of his children. Yet never once has he asked me one question about my family. Although I have to say God really uses him, the self-centeredness shouts so loud, that it is hard to hear what he is saying.

It also depicts a pitiful prayer life. If one is not interested in anyone but himself when you talk to him in person, guess whom he prays for when He talks to God?

Most people I counsel who have serious ongoing problems are extremely self-centered people. They see only themselves at the center of the universe. The more their thoughts dwell on themselves, the more negative they become. It is gross immaturity, and is the beginning of mental illness.

Positive people rarely talk about themselves. They have learned not to turn their eyes inward, and have broken free from the detestable bondage of self-centeredness. There is absolutely nothing more lonely than the prison of self-centeredness. Who wants to enter that world with you?

Delivered From a Negative Spirit

There is a demon that is simply a negative demon. Some people seem to have been 'plugged in' negative at birth. To them the world is a place where things rarely go right. The tone in their voice has a whine to it, and worry is etched in every facial expression.

When you converse with negative people every positive word is batted down. It doesn't matter what you say, there will be a negative counter answer to neutralize your positive report.

These people, in order to get help, must want to change. They, themselves, must make a decision to seek deliverance. Many don't want to change. They enjoy being negative. It has become normal to them. But God is well able to deliver as soon as they totally desire freedom.

Negative People Wear Out the Saints

I am willing to stay up all night and pray with someone who wants help, but negative people weary me. Often they will attach themselves to someone who is positive, in order to get a temporary lift out of their negative zone. They are seeking relief, but they in fact need deliverance.

Those who are not seeking God, but only go about pursuing willing listeners, have become instruments to wear out the saints.

> 'And he shall speak great words against the most High, and shall **wear out** the saints of the most High . . .'
>
> (Daniel 7:25)

Negatively bound people don't always want to change.

Rather, they seek out relief and go from person to person to pour out their negative perspective of their tunnel-visioned life.

I've seen dating relationships where, for example, the young man is attracted to the girl because she is bubbly and positive and makes him feel good. But his negative spirit will eventually sap her strength and she will end up burdened in the relationship, always having to lift him out of his depression. I would counsel her to get out of the relationship, unless he fervently seeks deliverance (and gets it) because she will always have to fight that negative and burdensome blanket of oppression. I don't wish that on anyone.

Laziness

There is an inherent laziness on the part of the negative person. It is easier to swallow the devil's negative merchandise than to stand up and resist him. '... *Resist the devil and he will flee from you.*' (James 4:7) Instead, the passive and indolent nature begins to cower rather than fight, and seeks out someone to unload on, or something to make him feel better. But this cycle can be broken through the power of God, if the person really wants to be free. Jesus came to set the captive free.

Frankly, all growth in God requires exercise. Just as physical strength comes from exercise, so does spiritual strength. And it is easier to talk about exercise than to do it.

That is why some people would rather 'rehash' their problems over and over, rather than exercise their faith in God by resisting the lies of the devil and declaring the word of God to every mountain in their path.

Yeah, But ...

The most common words I hear when I counsel 'plugged-in-negative' people are 'Yeah, but ...' It doesn't matter what kind of positive and hopeful declaration you make, you can rest assured you will soon hear a 'Yeah, but ...'

When people are still saying 'Yeah, but ...' they are still

in the analytical stage. No one will receive anything from God by analyzing. It has to be received by faith. The analytical, natural or carnal mind was not created to receive from God.

> *'For to be carnally minded is death, but to be spiritually minded is life and peace. Because the carnal mind is enmity (hostile) against God; for it is not subject to the law of God, nor indeed can be.'*
>
> (Romans 8:6–7)

The word, carnal, means meat or flesh. In other words the carnal mind means a meat-mind or 'meat-head.' I always remind myself that when I begin to analyze God instead of obey His Spirit, I am becoming spiritually a 'meathead.'

Fear has Torment

There are two basic emotions in life, fear and love. So many people are tormented by evil spirits, but the root of all torment is fear. Fear is the avenue where tormenting spirits get their feet in the door.

But God has made provision! His love. He desires that we allow Him to saturate our being with His love so there is literally no room for fear.

> *'Love has been perfected among us in this: that we may have boldness in the day of judgment: because as He is, so are we in this world. **There is no fear in love; but perfect love casts out fear, because fear involves torment.** But he who fears has not been made perfect in love. We love Him because He first loved us.'*
>
> (1 John 4:17–19)

Any voice you hear, or think you hear, that does not resound with love is not from God. **All** thoughts from the devil involve fear and torment.

Demons Can be Convincing

Having been a victim of torment much of my life, I have great compassion when someone is being lied to by an evil spirit; it is a very real experience.

There is a way that evil spirits persuasively penetrate the thought life that makes a lie seem like the truth. (I guess they've had a lot of practice). I can speak with empathy because there have been times when, under attack, those spirits made me think I was miserable, when I really wasn't.

It is not necessarily a situation of hearing voices (as when a convicted criminal claims a voice told him to do it) rather it is being overwhelmed with negative thoughts. It seems as though it's momentarily impossible to see anything positive.

I like to describe it as a person 'under' a spirit. It is easy to recognize it in one-on-one counselling. For example, someone whom I have talked with previously about taking authority over evil spirits, will call. I can recognize immediately that he is 'under' an evil spirit (not possessed, but being oppressed). There is a definite difference in his voice, as if he is trying to talk with someone standing on his chest. There is not a hint of victory in any word he says.

In fact, when I get these calls, I feel like my heart falls into my shoe laces because I know that I am going to have to talk firmly and confront this person. Once again, he has let a host of evil spirits get into his thinking.

This person is 'under' a spirit. The reason he is under a spirit is due to entertaining lies at some point. For example, perhaps he had a disappointing experience, such as a discouraging evaluation at work. Rather than live the life of praising God in the midst of his disappointment, he began to entertain doubts of God's goodness and, quickly, demons saw the open door and rushed in to 'help'. The devil will swiftly accommodate anyone who is willing to turn his eyes inward and accentuate the negative.

It usually begins with questions like, 'Where is God?' 'I've prayed and I've prayed, and still haven't seen a breakthrough.' 'I'm just a failure – I don't understand what God has against me.'

Soon this person is inundated with defeat. The only solution is for him to **resist** the lies, and begin to speak with his **own** mouth the faithfulness of God, and declare His Word.

Normal Christianity is a life of praise. We literally have to wear praise as a garment at all times. '... *The garment of praise for the spirit of heaviness.*' (Isaiah 61:3)

When we begin to complain, or accuse God, or emphasize the negative, we are doing nothing but removing the garment of praise, as someone who takes off a coat on a cold day. Even if you don't understand what is going on, praise and thankfulness are as a **protection** from the enemy.

David made a classic and all inclusive statement that pertains to every believer.

> '*I will bless the Lord **at all times**. His praise shall continually be in my mouth.*'
>
> (Psalm 34:1)

Demons That Come and Go, and Swap Places

God wants us free from torment at all times. If you resist the evil spirits that have harassed you in times past, you are making progress. However, I have noticed a pattern in the way that evil spirits try to return to harass.

We all have weak areas and, of course, the enemy is a dirty fighter who attacks us in those weakest areas. Even though we have recognized the crack in our armor and have rebuked the devil (experiencing a certain degree of victory) there will be times when these oppressors, like persistent and annoying salesmen, will arrive at our doorstep. They will once again try to gain entry. After all, they did 'enjoy' a fairly effective occupation at one time.

This is where you have to be strong and quickly recognize the symptoms, **that come in the form of negative thinking** and refuse to entertain the thoughts – even momentarily. As you resist diabolical thoughts, you will observe the frequency of attacks begins to lessen.

Additionally, demons will switch places. You may be tormented all week in one area, then suddenly that 'area' doesn't bother you any more. However, the torment begins in another area. For example, a person may be tormented for weeks about his job. He will go through all kinds of mental anguish over something about his job. Then suddenly he is not tormented about that any more, but he will begin to be tormented about something totally unrelated to what bothered him before. The same tormenting spirits (spirits of discontent) have just switched areas.

Once this person can recognize this 'cat and mouse' game the devil is playing, he can rebuke the root of the problem. The **root** of the problem is a tormenting spirit of discontent.

Buyer's Remorse

One sure way to discern whether or not you are being tormented by an evil spirit, is if the attack is focussed on something you **cannot personally change**. People who are more susceptible to torment always get hit hardest in this area. The cruelty of this type of torment is in that it most always follows a commitment or a decision. Most often, it is not until the decision is final, that the remorseful thoughts come flooding in. This is pure torment (never from the Lord) as the devil is trying to rob the person of the joy of the moment.

The fact that thoughts are coming regarding something that is irreversible, is a guarantee that the thoughts are from the devil.

God **never** torments people. He will never give you thoughts regarding irreversible decisions. He will, however, give insight on how to rectify situations.

Most people have experienced buyer's remorse at some point in their lives. Once a purchase has been made, it is a sinking feeling to experience the remorse begin to pour in. To those susceptible, I would encourage them to bind the evil spirit before you go into the store, or contemplate the finality of a purchase. The devil has found a point of weakness in you that he can use to rob your joy.

The devil is a joy robber, so any time you make a decision, he will come immediately to you with thoughts that you picked the wrong color, or you are too extravagant, or any tormenting thought he can get you to listen to. Wise up! The devil is simply trying to rob the joy of living. Rebuke him! Besides, no one is perfect. We all make wrong decisions from time to time.

Similarly, there is another classification of torment which I like to refer to as 'obeyer's remorse'. Any time you step out in faith and obey God, immediately opposing thoughts will come. Usually this is just good 'confirmation' that you did indeed obey God.

The bottom line is that the devil is going to try to steal your joy. He can't keep you from belonging to God, so he lies and steals, to keep you miserable. Rebuke him in Jesus' Name.

Tough Hide!

An old preacher approached me once. I had known him for a number of years. 'I was praying for you,' he said, 'and the Lord showed me that He has toughened your hide. The enemy cannot affect you in those areas that he used to be able to.'

He was hearing from God. I knew that, for a significant period of time, I had not been tormented in any of the familiar areas. The Lord had indeed toughened me. To God be the glory!

It doesn't always work just to rebuke the enemy one time or to be ministered to once. Thank God for every special experience, but we also must **walk** in the knowledge we have gained. Our walk must be **consistent** in resisting lies, exalting the Lord, and confessing His Word. Growth and strength come through exercising authority out of **our own spirit**.

Many don't understand this. When others minister to you, it is very encouraging and uplifting. Individual ministry helps you to clarify your problem, and strengthens you to a point, helping you to 'get your head above water.' However, the real and permanent growth comes when you, yourself, **exercise** authority over the enemy. No one gains muscle by watching someone else lift weights. It may be inspiring to watch, but growth comes with doing the exercise yourself.

We have to be on guard against the 'lazy' mentality. Every individual is accountable for himself and must do his part. How easy it is to let someone else do the praying, the resisting, and the overcoming.

But God wants you and me as individuals to grow strong. There will be no growth without opposition and resistance.

God loves the overcomer. You do not have to be a Christian long to realize walking in the Spirit involves overcoming. Through the act of overcoming, God gives new authority and strength.

> *'He who overcomes, I will make him a **pillar** in the temple of My God.'*
>
> (Revelation 3:12)

The weakest area in your life, when submitted to God, becomes your strongest area. For instance, if a chair has a wobbly leg, and you have it repaired, it becomes the strongest leg. Our areas of weakness become potential areas for the glory of God to be revealed.

Double-Mindedness

I used to think that a double-minded man was a man who said one thing one day, then changed his mind and voiced another belief another day. For example, someone promises the pastor to help paint the church, and then doesn't show up. That doesn't make him double-minded, but rather a liar.

A double-minded man is one who believes one thing on the inside of him, but declares with his mouth something different.

He is a man with two minds. His spirit mind has a belief, but his natural man does not agree with the belief of his spirit-man, but rather of his emotions.

In other words, a double-minded man believes one thing, but says another.

Double-mindedness guarantees that you will receive little from God.

> *'But let him ask in faith, with no doubting, for he who*

*doubts is like a wave of the sea driven and tossed by the wind. For let not that man suppose that he will receive anything from the Lord; he is a **double-minded man, unstable in all his ways.***'

(James 1:6–8)

Living the Life

Many people are tormented because they are living on the fence. They are not totally committed to the gospel and living for the increase of the kingdom of God. They continue to view the gospel as a way of relief from their problems, rather than living a transformed, crucified and Spirit-led life.

Fence-sitting is a miserable existence, because you are divided between two masters; what your flesh and sensual desires demand, and the surrendered life that the Holy Spirit requires.

Above All ... Be Thankful

Take time to count your blessings! There is something about a thankful person that keeps the blessings of God flowing.

A thankful heart is a protection from the onslaughts of the enemy. Gratitude and thanksgiving keep tormenting thoughts at bay.

Those who refuse to be thankful, and complain continually, greatly hinder the blessings of God that He desires to send their way.

> *'And let the peace of God rule in your hearts, to which also you were called in one body; and **be thankful**.'*
>
> (Colossians 3:15)

> *'Continue earnestly in prayer, being vigilant in it **with thanksgiving**.'*
>
> (Colossians 4:2)

> *'Neither filthiness, nor foolish talking, nor coarse jesting, which are not fitting, but rather **giving of thanks**.'*
>
> (Ephesians 5:4)

> *'Be anxious for nothing, but in everything by prayer and supplication, **with thanksgiving**, let your requests be made known to God.'*
>
> (Philippians 4:6)

These are truths the Lord spoke to my wife and I concerning thankfulness:

A thankful heart is a healthy heart.

Thankfulness brings health to the bones.

Thankfulness brings release to your spirit.

Thankfulness helps you focus on Kingdom motives.

Thankfulness helps you mount up on wings as the eagle.

Thankfulness is like medicine – it edifies the soul.

Thankfulness is where your breakthrough begins!

Chapter 7

Don't be Comfortable with Bondage

– People who are in religious bondage don't recognize it, because bondage that is ignored has been accepted as normal –

'Stand fast therefore in the liberty by which Christ has made us free, and do not be entangled again with a yoke of bondage.'

(Galatians 5:1)

When we first moved into a new neighborhood in our city, I was confident that our son, David, would soon find new friends in his junior high age bracket. However, after a number of months had passed, I recognized that God was up to something. All the neighbors' children within several blocks were either toddlers, or high school age. So it seemed I was his only friend (with the exception of his friends at school). I was the one who shot baskets and threw the football with him, and even (somewhat reluctantly) played video games.

At first it made me frustrated that in a neighborhood our size there was no companion for our son. But over the months of filling in the friendship gap with him, God began to reveal to me how, in like manner, He had worked with young David (the shepherd boy) before He exalted him to be king over Israel.

He began to disclose to me that in the same way I was our son's best friend, He was David's best friend.

God isolated David from his brothers by putting him in an environment where the Holy Spirit was his only companion. It was the wisdom of God to 'hide' David for a season of time. The Lord knew what He was doing. In order for David to fulfill the purpose of God, he had to come to know Him more intimately.

It is safe to say, that if it were left up to most of us, we would quickly surround ourselves with people, rather than spend time alone with the Lord. So God put David in that environment of sheep-watching, where he passed many hours fellowshipping with the Lord.

The Problem with Bondage

A common problem with Christians is that we become so comfortable with our environment and the people we are around, that we cease to live in an intimate relationship with God. It is very tempting to become people-centered and activity-centered rather than God-centered in our lives.

We easily settle into this type of bondage; the bondage of religious monotony and powerlessness. The reason is simple; we haven't sacrificed the time to know God.

One of the saddest aspects of human nature is that we can easily adapt to being comfortable in a state of religious bondage. Rather than defy a situation which may involve confrontation and temporary discomfort, we are guilty of compromise. For the sake of peace, we take the easiest route and let ourselves adjust and comply with something we don't agree with and are definitely not happy with. Although we are miserable, we do nothing. Bondage has become more acceptable than paying the price for truth and freedom.

David's Beginnings

It may have been easy to feel sorry for David as a young seventeen-year old shepherd boy. Here he was doing the boring part, watching his father's sheep, while his brothers were off traveling and involved in an exciting battle. I'm sure he wanted to escape from that isolated place and join the escapades that his brothers were involved in.

Even when Samuel came to anoint God's chosen one to be the next king, and had prayerfully examined each of his brothers as a prospect, David's name was only brought up as a remote possibility that could hardly be taken seriously.

> *'And Samuel said to Jesse, "Are all the young men here?" Then he said, "There remains yet the youngest, and there he is, keeping the sheep."'*
>
> (1 Samuel 16:11)

But **God knew who David was,**

> *'And Samuel said to Jesse, "Send and bring him. For we will not sit down till he comes here." So he sent and brought him in. Now he was ruddy, with bright eyes, and good looking. And the Lord said, "Arise, anoint him; for* **this is the one.***"'*
>
> (vs. 12)

Let Him Work a Good Work in You

When we find ourselves in situations similar to David's, our first inclination is to complain. We have a tendency to feel as though God has been unfair to us. But I contend that when God's hand is on your life, He may well 'hide' you for a season. He certainly hid Moses (forty years) and Paul (over three years).

God has a plan for the lives of each of us, as most Christians have heard again and again. But usually our prayer is for God to create the fastest possible exit from our present situation. The reason we pray for these fast exits is we lack a vision of preparation. Once we begin to recognize we are in preparation, peace and contentment come.

David wasn't missing out when he was caring for the sheep and his brothers were in more exciting 'ministry.' **He was in preparation!**

His preparation was the same as the preparation that God requires for each of us today. We must become worshippers of God, and come to know God. Can you see the wisdom of God, that He had to isolate David from his brothers and keep him in a situation where he had no one to fellowship with but God alone?

A Poor Substitute

Usually, if it left up to us as individuals, we will do more fellowshipping with people than with God. How easy it is to become people-dependent rather than Holy Spirit-dependent.

This situation is compounded by the fact that there are so many activities available for each of us to get involved in. You don't have to be a new convert for long, to realize that keeping busy won't be a problem.

This is the first derailment from an intimate walk with the Lord that a new Christian faces. It is astoundingly easy to become activity-centered and oriented, rather than obedient to Jesus. Tragically, the first thing churches often do with the newly converted is to put them to work. What is needed first and foremost is to help the new babe in Christ develop intimacy with the Holy Spirit.

Friends, or any religious activities, are **never** to be a substitute in exchange for God Himself! There is a restlessness in all of us initially when it comes to being alone – with God. Whether we are nervous, bored, impatient, sleepy, or frustrated, we still have a need to learn to be comfortable in the presence of God – alone.

Listening to the Spirit or learning to 'wait' on God in His presence, is a discipline which must be encouraged and developed in each of us, for true growth to come forth. It is a discipline which contradicts our soulish desires, but enhances our spiritual man. Our prayer life is not to be a chore or obligation, but a privilege and joy. In reality, it is the most exciting, stimulating and enlightening place in the universe to be.

Don't Call a Friend

Even James writes

> *'Is any among you suffering (afflicted)? Let him pray. Is anyone cheerful? Let him sing psalms.'*
>
> (James 5:13)

Notice he does not say that if anyone is suffering (this doesn't pertain to physical sickness) let him call his friends and talk to them about it. He says, if someone is afflicted with a problem, to pray! In other words, go to God – first! Express your frustration regarding your problem to Him. Let Him be your best friend. Ventilate your feelings first to Him. Maybe He had to allow the 'affliction' to get your attention so you would draw near to Him.

But how easy it is to stiff-arm the Holy Spirit. Rather than seeing Him as our source, we quickly dial the phone of a friend, or drop by a friend's house. We think nothing of spending exorbitant amounts on long-distance calls to express our need to someone we love, and yet the Holy Spirit patiently waits. He'll wait all your life (He has more time than you do) because His ultimate purpose is that you and I come to know Him.

> *'But let him who glories glory in this, that he understands and **knows** Me . . .'*
>
> (Jeremiah 9:23)

Some people have to have a close friend to whom they tell everything. They may be on the phone numerous times a day with this special person. Sometimes it appears as though they are addicted to the friendship, rather than just having someone to enjoy. These people usually never see or acknowledge this weakness, but tremendous spiritual growth comes when they do. It is amazing that we may spend two to thre hours of a day in phone conversations with friends, and only minutes with the Holy Spirit. Of course it is not wrong to have a good friend, as long as the Holy Spirit is your best friend.

Then James continues, *'Is anyone cheerful? Let him sing psalms.'* Notice he doesn't say to let him testify at church, or to call everyone he knows and tell of his victory. First, when you have a victory, or if the Lord has flooded you with joy, express it to Him! Ventilate your joys and jubilation to Him. First!

Again, it is not wrong to have friends and to tell them of our problems and victories. But the Holy Spirit desires that He remains first, above our friends.

The Buddy Vacuum

Every person has a 'buddy vacuum.' The desire of countless people is to have that close friend whom they can confide in.

But the Holy Spirit wants to be your buddy. He is to be the Christian's closest friend. It is easy to substitute a person to fill the need in our hearts rather than the Holy Spirit. It is in this area where sincere people compromise more than any other area.

I used to wonder why I went through various things in my life. As a new Christian and a freshman in college, I quickly saw my old high school buddies disappear after they heard of my commitment to Christ. I prayed for friends constantly, but for an entire year friends never came. Then I transferred to a Christian college for one year, where I made plenty of friends, but still there remained a void within me. The following year I transferred back to my state university, and spent a lot of hours of loneliness once again. It wasn't until well into my senior year that suddenly I was inundated with friends. These fellow students came to me asking questions about the baptism in the Holy Spirit, and other topics from Scripture. In the following months more than a dozen of them were filled with the Holy Spirit.

Looking back upon this period of my life, I regret all the time I spent in prayer asking God for friends. I clearly see what the desire of the Lord was. He wanted me to cultivate friendship with Him! He wanted to be my closest friend. Not only did He want to fill within me that God-sized vacuum that St. Augustine described (God has put a God-sized vacuum in every man); He also wanted to fill that buddy-sized vacuum that He had created within me. To further elaborate, the God-size vacuum within us is filled or satisfied when we have a salvation encounter with God. But the buddy-size vacuum is only satisfied through personal intimacy with the Holy Spirit.

In my ignorance, of course, I prayed asking God to send me friends, yet He wanted me to pray that I would first let Him fill every fiber of my being. After which, of course, He would send friends across my path.

> *'But seek first the kingdom of God and His righteousness, and all these things shall be added to you.'*
>
> (Matthew 6:33)

Occupy Till He Comes

Fresh out of college I was instructed by the Lord to *'Occupy till I come'* (see Luke 19:13). This, of course, meant to just do the natural thing until He revealed what spiritual thing He had called me to. It is a great temptation to run ahead of God at this point in our lives. Occupying is always frustrating to our flesh. However, there is great fruit produced in our lives when we wait upon the Lord. Usually it takes much more faith to **not** do something than to do it. I was fortunate in those early years of walking with the Lord, to be around seasoned Christians who warned me of the pitfalls of trying to establish my own ministry, with my own energy, and with my own understanding.

God Wants to Hide You; You're His Best Kept Secret

David was a prime example of the fact that God exercises the right to keep you a secret if He so desires. Although God had great plans for David, God chose to hide him. He, being the youngest, was tending the sheep while his brothers were doing more exciting things on the front lines of the battle.

However, God had His purposes. David was alone, without friends and companionship, but he was also **without distractions**. He was in a position to learn to know the Father.

If God had not placed David in that position, he no doubt would have sought out companionship to fill the void with Him. But he would have missed learning to know God the way he did. God knows best how to deal with our human nature.

Few people seek God because they simply **want** to know Him. The majority of the human race come to God because they **need** Him.

Friends Can Be a Substitute

If David had been in a comfortable situation where he was in constant contact and fellowship with his brothers, that 'comfortable' state would have robbed him of being in intimate communion with God! No doubt God arranges such times in our lives where our flesh desires companionship, yet the Lord hides us unto Himself, where we learn to draw from Him. If we are not careful, we can become so people-centered that we are perpetually distracted from hearing the voice of the Lord. Rather than complaining about those times of loneliness, we can learn to cultivate fellowship with the Father. He loves us enough to keep us in a hidden state for a season in our lives.

If we are not careful, we will fight against the Holy Spirit through our insistence to fellowship with people first, rather than God. Others will never satisfy that buddy-size vacuum that God has placed within us.

Many who were destined to do great things for God have refused to let Him deal with this area, and have let the desire for friends and fellowship override a more intimate encounter with God.

Know No One After the Flesh

One of the most difficult things to learn in our Christian walk is that our fellowship with one another is to be in the Spirit.

Paul exhorted the Christians this way,

> *'Therefore, from now on, we regard no one according to
> the flesh. Even though we have known Christ according
> to the flesh, yet now we know Him thus no longer.'*
> (2 Corinthians 5:16)

Quite frankly, so much of our prayers come from the
desire of our flesh and not of the Spirit. We want God to give
us friends that appeal to our likes and dislikes.

But knowing people after the Spirit, is far more exciting.
In other words, our fellowship is centered around what God
is saying by His Spirit, and not our fleshly interests. In a
sense, it is the Holy Spirit in me, in fellowship with the Holy
Spirit in you. Of course it doesn't mean that there will not be
conversations and events around natural things, but what
ultimately binds us together is the fellowship of the Spirit.

One brother in particular who lives in another part of the
United States, is a great blessing to me. Every couple of
years when we see each other, we both just embrace and
laugh. Each of us in our spirits feel such joy. Then as we
converse, it is as if we've never been apart. Our fellowship is
of the Spirit. I am always so edified, just being in this
brother's presence.

God wants all of our relationships to be that way. We
know one another after the Spirit, as He communicates His
mind to both of us. Talk about edifying conversation!

No longer is conversation merely in a golf game, or what
color we painted the den, or the type of landscaping we did
(there is nothing wrong with these things) but rather what
the Holy Spirit is speaking into our lives.

An Exercise in Hating Bondage

Before God began to exalt David, He took him through a lot
of training. David had learned to fellowship with God, and
had become a worshipper of God. He understood the presence of the Lord and had learned how to abide in His
presence.

The Lord assigned David an exercise in hating bondage.
Having an intolerance for bondage is one of the first things
we have to learn in order to minister effectively.

When Saul was tormented by evil spirits, David was appointed to sing and play for him, and drive away the evil spirits.

> *'But the Spirit of the Lord departed from Saul, and a distressing spirit from the Lord troubled him. And Saul's servants said to him, "Surely, a distressing spirit from God is troubling you. Let our master now command your servants, who are before you, to seek out a man who is a skillful player on the harp. And it shall be that he will play it with his hand when the distressing spirit from God is upon you, and you shall be well."'*

(1 Samuel 16:14–16)

> *'Then one of the servants answered and said, "Look, I have seen a son of Jesse, the Bethlehemite, who is skillful in playing, a mighty man of valor, a man of war, prudent in speech, and a handsome person; and the Lord is with him."'*

(vs. 18)

> *'And so it was, whenever the spirit from God was upon Saul, that David would take a harp and play with his hand. Then Saul would become refreshed and well, and the distressing spirit would depart from him.'*

(vs. 23)

This is the first thing God teaches us. We must become first of all, worshippers. Worship brings the presence of God. As a result we learn to be in tune with Him. This can no longer be considered an option for a few super saints. Normal Christianity is living a life as a true worshipper, and being led by the Spirit of God. *'For as many as are led by the Spirit of God, these are the Sons of God.'* (Romans 8:14) Sons are those who have come into maturity and have **embraced a lifestyle of listening to the Holy Spirit**.

The more we live as worshippers, the less value we put on fleshly accomplishments.

'For we are the circumcision, who worship God in the Spirit, and rejoice in Christ Jesus, and have no confidence in the flesh.'

(Philippians 3:3)

It was no accident that David was 'discovered' to be the appointed one to sing over Saul. If you pay the price to know God, you will be sought out. This world needs people who know God and who have learned how to commune with Him.

'A man's gift makes room for him, and brings him before great men.'

(Proverbs 18:16)

Before we do great things for God, we have to learn to cultivate fellowship with Him in our own spirit. If we don't know how to exercise victory in our own spirit, we can offer little strength to others. It is in fellowship with God that we learn to subject our fleshly habits and desires to Him.

This is a higher priority in God's eyes than conquering great cities and accomplishing great things. He first wants to set up communion and be Lord in our personal life.

'He who is slow to anger is better than the mighty, and he who rules his spirit than he who takes a city.'

(Proverbs 16:32)

You'll Either be Comfortable With the Presence of God or With Bondage

When David's father sent him to the front lines to check on his brothers and bring food to them, he probably had no inkling that he was going to be placed in the battle.

But God had established his presence in David. **David was more familiar with the anointing than he was with bondage**. There is no record that David sensed any fear. Rather He was filled with disdain! The intimidating defiant statements of Goliath were in great contrast to the presence of the Lord

119

that David was familiar with. In fact there is indication of shock in his reaction that his brothers were putting up with this situation. David's anointed declaration was as follows,

> *'What shall be done for the man who kills this Philistine and takes away the reproach from Israel?* **For who is this uncircumcised Philistine, that he should defy the armies of the living God?'**

(1 Samuel 17:26)

David felt disdain in his spirit toward bondage. His brothers only felt fear. They had become more comfortable with bondage since that is what they were familiar with. All their fellowship had been with one another (they fed each other's fears) instead of individual communion with a (fearless) God.

Churches are full of saints who once embraced the presence of God, but have slowly settled into comfortable bondage. They at one time were appalled when the Spirit was quenched and not allowed to move, but now their senses have been dulled. The problem being, if you stay in a dead church long enough, you'll begin to like it! If you stay around bondage long enough, you will become comfortable with it.

But fellowship with the Holy Spirit will keep you intolerant of bondage.

The Lions and the Bears

When David stood before Saul, and offered to fight the Philistine, Saul replied,

> *'You are not able to go against this Philistine to fight with him; for you are but a youth, and he a man of war from his youth.'*

(1 Samuel 16:33)

It was interesting that David had to **convince** the leadership that God was able to overcome Goliath. He indeed had the mind of the Lord, while Saul was as intimidated as everyone else.

> *'Your servant used to keep his father's sheep, and when a lion or a bear came and took a lamb out of the flock, I went out after it and struck it, and delivered the lamb from its mouth; and when it arose against me, I caught it by the beard, and struck it and killed it. Your servant has killed both lion and bear; and this uncircumcised Philistine will be like one of them, seeing he has defied the armies of the living God.'*
>
> (vs. 30)

> *'Moreover David said, "The Lord, who delivered me from the paw of the lion and from the paw of the bear, He will deliver me from the hand of this Philistine."'*
>
> (vs. 37)

Before we see God doing great things through us, He prepares us. Part of the preparation is dealing with the lions and bears in our lives.

It was a number of years from the time Samuel anointed David until God exalted him as king. But those years were priceless, because they were years of preparing David for God's purpose. Although David was being faithful (as many people are) he saw no immediate manifestation to match his kingly anointing. But God was developing the manifestation of character on the **inside**.

God begins His work on the inside of us. Before we are sent to the front lines in public, He has us work on the 'back lines' in private.

On the 'back lines' we all have lions and bears that have to be dealt with.

> *'Therefore humble yourselves under the mighty hand of God, that He may exalt you* **in due time**.*'*
>
> (1 Peter 5:6)

You Can't Fight the Goliaths in Public Until You Confront the Lions and Bears in Private

It is no accident that David had to kill both a lion and a bear, as he was watching the sheep.

121

In the privacy of our personal relationship with God, the Holy Spirit will join us in the confrontation of the lions and bears that exist in our lives.

Although David was still a very young man, he had been through some things. With no one to help him and no one to admire his steadfastness and endurance, he had to depend totally upon God to overcome these great obstacles. No doubt he had to overcome fear more than anything.

The lions and bears in our lives are no accident. They are the testing and proving ground of our character. There are no short cuts to maturity. God requires us to face the lions and bears in our personal lives before He launches us into any public ministry.

Sheep watching doesn't seem like a very exciting ministry, but it is in caring for the sheep that we learn patience and cultivate compassion. There is nothing more hollow than listening to someone minister who doesn't really care about people. Some leaders (who seem to like crowds, but don't like people) severely lack compassion. When any ministry lacks compassion, I question the call of God on his or her life. God requires that the quality of compassion be preeminent in our lives. Oftentimes, preceding many miracles, Jesus was first moved with compassion. '... *but faith working through love.*' (Galatians 5:6) I suppose the devil can counterfeit a lot of things, but he cannot counterfeit compassion.

Great have been the falls of leaders, who have first neglected or ignored their lions and bears before they entered public ministry.

David wasn't attempting to be labelled as a lion killer, he just loved sheep! It was out of caring for the sheep that David had to rescue them from the mouth of the lion or bear.

Sometimes it seems we are seeking a personal ministry instead of just seeking the will of God. Showing compassion right where you are, is the best ministry anyone can have, and the beginning of greater ministry.

The Lions in Our Lives

We all have lions in our lives. Naturally, they come in different forms, but I perceive the most prominent lion that we all face is rebellion. It is interesting that the word, rebellion, can be divided into those two words, rebel and lion.

We all have to confront that rebellious nature that is innate in every human being. Just being saved, or filled with the Holy Spirit, doesn't guarantee that we don't have rebellion within us.

The true test is when the Holy Spirit confronts us, or lets someone (he uses people) interfere with our plans. It is easy to serve God, as long as He never contradicts our own will. But when the Holy Spirit starts tampering with our rights, that is another story.

When that old lion of rebellion rises up, he has to be faced, conquered, and killed. Until he is dealt with, we are not ready for ministry. Many great men of God publicly failed God and faced national humiliation, quite possibly because a lion in their personal lives was never dealt with and put to death.

The lion can come in many other forms, lust, greed, and the desire for power and recognition, etc. There are many. But the bottom line is that the Holy Spirit doesn't just want to come in our lives and guide us during times of special need and direction, rather He wants to come in and **possess** our lives!

The Bears in Our Lives

The bears in our lives must also be confronted. We must have victory over the bears, before we are ready for ministry. Bears can be likened to the spirit of fear, discouragement, despondency, pouting, self-pity, melancholy, depression, and all the highs and lows of emotions that rule us. We can be high on God for a while, and totally depressed an hour later. That old bear in our nature has to be confronted, dealt with, and put to death. The flesh loves the bear. It is easier to agree with the bear, to give in to the emotions, to embrace defeat, rather than walk in victory.

Bear killing is difficult. We love to feel sorry for ourselves. We like to accentuate the negative, and dwell on the past. But that old bear has to go to the cross. There is no other place for him.

We Must Be More Comfortable With the Anointing Than With Bondage

When young David approached the battle lines, he was free from fear for one reason. He was more acclimatized to the presence of the Lord, than he was with fear and unbelief. His spirit was immediately provoked because what he saw and heard was in such contradiction to the Spirit of God within him. All those hours watching the sheep were not wasted hours.

Many have heard it preached that the Christian's main job in life is to get out and save the world. We often neglect to mention that first we must come to know the Father, and be intimate with the Holy Spirit. How ignorant it is to accuse God of not putting us into some type of ministry so we can help Him do His work. **Our first ministry is unto Him**.

> *'But the people who **know their God** shall be strong, and carry out great exploits.'*
>
> (Daniel 11:32b)

When Human Ambition Begins to Die, the Ministry is Coming Forth

It is not wrong to desire to be used by God. But we cannot allow the humanness in us to get in God's way. We must be broken vessels, in order for His light to come through. If we have not let God crucify the human ambition and motive in us, all that will become manifest is pride, arrogance and manufactured authority.

There is nothing more repulsive than pride and ego. When someone ministers publicly, and humility and brokenness is lacking, you can guarantee that very little of the Holy Spirit is coming through. But when God has done a work in a person, it is evidence, because the glory of God is coming through. He is glorified!

Shine on, Lord!

Chapter 8

Overcoming Discouragement

– Discouraged people exert no demand on the presence of God –

> *'And they overcame him by the blood of the Lamb and by the word of their testimony, and they did not love their lives unto death.'*
>
> (Revelation 12:11)

Recently my wife and I were ministering in a conference in a northern city. The night before we were to speak, the Lord spoke to my wife in a dream. In the dream, she was in a restaurant, where there was a smorgasbord-type eating arrangement. As people filed in, there was a huge sign that couldn't be missed that read, 'Buy this.' Then as she looked at the food on the smorgasbord, each portion of various 'food' was marked with a little tiny sign that was deceptively difficult to read.

Each food portion was labeled with such words as unbelief, sickness, disease, discouragement, and depression. Those in line were totally unaware of the deception they were falling for. One by one they began filling their trays up with helpings of all these separate bowls. They were buying the sickness and the discouragement and the unbelief. Then she saw herself at the end of the line near the cash register, helplessly watching the people fill their trays. Suddenly a person, whom she instantly knew was the Holy Spirit, came up behind her and said, 'Tell them about the blood of Jesus.' 'Remind them about the blood of Jesus.' Then she woke up.

As she lay there pondering the dream, she saw the reality of what the Lord was saying. The blood of Jesus is all encompassing. All physical health, all mental health, all emotional health has been purchased by the blood of Jesus. His precious blood not only paid for our sins, but for every possible sickness as well. In fact Jesus paid for our sicknesses with His blood **before** He paid for our sins. '... *by His stripes you were healed.*' (1 Peter 2:24) He paid not only for our sins, but for our mental health. His blood covers the oppression that comes against our minds. His blood covers those distorted emotions because of things we've gone through. We don't have to buy unbelief, we don't have to buy the lies of depression, we don't have to succumb to anything, because the blood of Jesus has paid it all.

> '*And **they** overcame him by the blood of the Lamb and by the word of their testimony, and they did not love their lives unto death.*'
>
> (Revelation 12:11)

The devil is a liar. Presumably the most effective weapon he uses against the saints is discouragement. There is nothing more diabolical than those stifling feelings of heaviness that border on hopelessness. But the good news is that we have **already** been given authority over him.

> '*Now I heard a voice saying in heaven, "**Now** salvation, and strength, and the kingdom of our God, and the power of His Christ have come, for the accuser of our brethren, who accused them before our God day and night, **has been cast down**."*'
>
> (Revelation 12:10)

Stop Trying to Defeat the Devil

You cannot defeat the devil! He has already been defeated. His time has already come. He has been stripped of his power and authority. He only has the 'power' to lie and oppress. We have the authority through the blood of Jesus to resist his lies, and not to buy the defeat he tries to sell us.

> *'Having disarmed principalities and powers, He made a public spectacle of them, triumphing over them in it.'*
> (Colossians 2:15)

A mistake commonly made by many Christians is that they are still trying to fight an enemy that has already been defeated. Nowhere does the Scripture tell us to defeat the devil, but rather to **resist** him, and to exercise the authority that we have already been given over him. *'Therefore submit to God. **Resist** the devil and he will flee from you.'* (James 4:7)

Yet countless books are written which usually have some cleverly drawn satanic symbol on the cover, leaving the reader with the ominous impression that somehow there is a teetering and questionable victory yet to be won.

These type of books undermine the power of God and greatly obscure what Jesus has already accomplished on the cross.

Our efforts need to be concentrated not on defeating a defeated devil, but rather defeating our own flesh.

> *'**For the flesh lusts against the Spirit, and the Spirit against the flesh;** and these are contrary to one another, so that you do not do the things that you wish.'*
> (Galatians 5:17)

Our flesh needs to be brought under subjection to the Holy Spirit. It can only be done by yielding ourselves to the power of the Holy Spirit.

> *'For if you live according to the flesh you will die; but if **by the Spirit** you put to death the deeds of the body, you will live.'*
> (Romans 8:13)

The Devil Fights Through Deception

Until a Christian has the revelation that the devil has already been defeated, he will be spending needless energy exerting labor and struggling against a defeated foe.

But when the revelation comes that the devil is already defeated, the Christian only has to walk in the light and let the light of God expose all deception.

Darkness is no hazard or intimidation to light. When light comes, darkness flees.

Deception is darkness. When someone is in deception, he does not see light. But prayer changes things. Prayer will cause the light of God to expose deception in that person.

While we are in no way commanded to defeat the devil, we are commanded to walk in the light.

'For you were once darkness, but now you are light in the Lord. Walk as children of light.'

(Ephesians 5:8)

'But if we walk in the light as He is in the light, we have fellowship with one another, and the blood of Jesus Christ His son cleanses us from all sin.'

(1 John 1:7)

'You are sons of light and sons of the day. We are not of the night nor of darkness.'

(1 Thessalonians 5:5)

'But you are a chosen generation, a royal priesthood, a holy nation, His own special people, that you may proclaim the praises of Him who called you out of darkness into His marvelous light.'

(1 Peter 2:9)

'The night is far spent, the day is at hand. Therefore let us cast off the works of darkness, and let us put on the armor of light.'

(Romans 13:12)

Stop Putting the Devil and God in the Same Arena

Another common misconception by Christians is that God and the devil are in some kind of spiritual boxing ring battling it out for a pending victory. Nothing could be farther from the truth. In fact, it is ridiculous to even make such a comparison. God is in no way on the same plateau as the devil. Heaven is His throne and the earth is His footstool (Isaiah 66:1).

At Calvary, Jesus purchased with His own blood as the righteous Lamb of God, our lost souls. This was in no way to pay a debt to the devil, but rather to pay the price God required, to redeem man from his sin. God has cut a covenant with man through the precious shed blood of Jesus.

Any claim the devil had on any human soul was lost at Calvary. Now we have access to God through the blood of Jesus, and we can come boldly.

> '*Therefore brethren, having boldness to enter the Holiest by the blood of Jesus.*'
>
> (Hebrews 10:19)

This covenant is between God and man, and has nothing to do with the devil. At Calvary, the devil was stripped of what he thought he had.

That is why Christians don't need to pray for power, but for light! As we walk in the light, we readily recognize that all things are ours, because we have been called into covenant with God, Himself.

> '*Therefore let no one boast in men. **For all things are yours**: whether Paul or Apollos or Cephas, or the world of life or death, or things present or things to come – all are yours. And you are Christ's, and Christ is God's.*'
>
> (1 Corinthians 3:21–23)

Victory Comes as We See From God's Perspective

Do you remember the experience of Elisha's servant? The king of Syria had made war against the king of Israel, and had sent horses and chariots and a great army to Dothan and surrounded the city. When the young man saw it, he was greatly afraid.

> *'And when the servant of the man of God arose early and went out, there was an army, surrounding the city with horses and chariots, and his servant said to him, "Alas, my master! What shall we do?"'*
>
> (1 Kings 6:15)

Elisha already had God's perspective.

> *'So he answered, "Do not fear, for those who are with us are more than those who are with them."'*
>
> (vs. 16)

Then the prophet simply prayed for the servant's eyes to be opened.

> *'And Elisha prayed, and said, "Lord, I pray, open his eyes that he may see." Then the Lord opened the eyes of the young man, and he saw. And behold the mountain was full of horses and chariots of fire all around Elisha.'*
>
> (vs. 17)

Nothing had changed! The enemy was still present. Circumstances were no different. When the servant's eyes were opened, and he saw the army of the Lord, suddenly there was nothing else to fear. We don't need more power over the devil! We already have it! What we need is our eyes to be open to see from God's perspective.

God doesn't want to change circumstances primarily. First He wants to open our eyes so that we can see from **His perspective**. Once our eyes are open, we clearly see that the enemy has already been defeated.

Many are walking in defeat, because they haven't heard the good news. The battle has already been won! Victory is already ours.

A soldier from World War II was found years later, still

surviving in the woods. He hadn't heard that the war was over. As soon as he heard the news, his perspective changed, and he returned to civilian life.

Many just need to hear good news. Jesus paid it. Jesus declared it, *'It is finished.'*

It was established before the foundation of the world. It was proclaimed at Calvary.

> *'. . . the Lamb slain from the foundation of the world.'*
> (Revelation 13:8)

Begin to Speak the Language of Faith

Many don't see victory because they refuse to embrace the language of faith. Speaking the language of faith is simply agreeing with God's vocabulary, and not the devil's.

It isn't enough to know the promises of God and the goodness of God. We must come to a place of choice. We can either stay in the rut we are in, or we can say, 'Enough is enough' and begin to speak what God says.

To the discouraged, God says, 'Choose life.' Begin to **agree** with God. Rather than declare your circumstances and what your emotions dictate, begin to declare the greatness of God!

It takes no faith (or character) to agree with your emotions. Emotions change by the minute. Anyone can declare the negative. Anyone can complain. Anyone can let his mouth spew out what his emotions feel at that given moment. Many spend their entire lives letting their vocal chords record what their emotions feel. But God has given you and me a choice.

> *'I call heaven and earth as witnesses today against you, that **I have set before you life and death, blessing and cursing; therefore choose life**, that both you and your descendants may live.'*
> (Deuteronomy 30:19)

God will wait for you to get tired of the old habitual rut

you are in. He will politely wait, and not stop you from wasting years. You can let it be your choice to continue plodding down the road of discouragement and despondency, and defeat. **Or**, you can **rise up in faith** and begin to speak His language. Without faith, it is impossible to please God. This is your choice.

The language of faith agrees with God. Faith declares God's faithfulness, and declares everything else a lie. You must not be concerned about what natural circumstances dictate, because from now on, God is your source. If things get worse at first, it doesn't matter, because God is seated on the throne of your life. Because you have begun to align your speech with His Word (speaking the language of faith), there will inevitably be results.

It is of necessity to repent. Repentance is not shedding a bucket of tears. Repentance simply means, about face! You must make a quality decision such as, 'I repent of agreeing with the devil's lies, I am choosing to agree with God, and speak His language.'

> *'Whoever offers praise glorifies Me; and to him who orders his conduct (conversation) aright **I will show** the salvation of God.'*
>
> (Psalm 50:23)

Fear is abnormal. God didn't create us to live in fear. Worry is abnormal. God didn't create us to live with worry. Joy is normal! Peace is normal! The gospel is good news which dictates our standard of living. Refuse to embrace fear and worry and discouragement. Embrace the promises of God! It is your choice.

Almost all suicides and suicide attempts can be traced back to the thought life. As choice was made a person began to entertain thoughts from the devil. The more the thoughts were listened to and entertained, the more thoughts the devil added. Soon the thoughts multiplied until the person could no longer control his own thoughts and tried to find a way of escape – by suicide. The problem began long before the suicide. The problem began when the person began to entertain the lies of the devil.

God has given you and me authority over **all** the power of the enemy.

> '*Behold, I give you the authority to trample on serpents and scorpions, and over all the power of the enemy, and nothing shall by any means hurt you.*'
>
> (Luke 10:19)

Gaining Strength by Resisting

I believe that the devil has a unique purpose. He is often used as a tool in the hand of God to make us stronger.

There is no way a person can gain strength without exercise, and all exercise involves resistance.

Health spas are very popular today. (They are also very expensive.) But when you enter the spa, all you see are numerous weights and exercise machines. The spa makes money selling you resistance!

Everyone knows that the only way to gain muscle and muscular strength is through resistance. That is why we willingly spend untold millions every year on health spas.

All exercise is resistance; whether it is lifting weights, bicycling, running, jogging, climbing mountains, or kicking the devil out of your way.

God knows that exercising our spirit through resistance to pressure and temptation, will bring growth and strength to our inner man.

That is why He commands us to resist the devil.

> '*Be sober, be vigilant; because your adversary the devil walks about like a roaring lion, seeking whom he may devour. **Resist him**, steadfast in the faith, knowing that the same sufferings are experienced by your brotherhood in the world.*'
>
> '*But may the God of all grace, who called us to His eternal glory by Christ Jesus, after you have suffered a while, perfect, establish, strengthen, and settle you.*'
>
> (1 Peter 5:8–10)

It isn't always God's way to rescue us from some type of

persecution or suffering. Sometimes He wants us to simply walk through it. As a result, He will perfect us, establish us, strengthen us, and settle us. Frankly, resisting the devil is what makes us steadfast in the faith.

God has a far greater purpose for us as individuals than we realize. He desires to make us strong in spirit. Strong Christians have gained strength by resisting the lies of the devil and by **exercising** their faith in God.

It is good to remind yourself when you are feeling satanic opposition and oppression, that you are **worth** being resisted! God has His hand on you.

No One Has Ever Become Strong by Watching Someone Else Exercise

It is so easy to talk about exercise and to even become stimulated and inspired watching someone work out. But the only way for you to benefit is to **do** the exercise yourself.

There is an element of laziness in all of us – in our flesh.

We all have a tendency to take short cuts. If there were only doctors who could prescribe medicine to make us strong. If there were only diets that allowed us to eat anything we want and lose weight. If there were only preachers that could preach so well that we would become powerful Christians, just by listening.

But there are no such things. Growing in God comes by becoming doers of the word and not hearers only (James 1:22).

Acting on the word, includes **resisting** the devil yourself. A small child may be oblivious to a bug crawling on his arm, and his mother has to brush the bug off. But as that child grows, he learns to brush off his own bugs, by exerting his **own** authority.

The devil is a bug that has to be brushed off. His lies have to be resisted.

However, some people would rather talk about the devil than resist him. Some like to rehash their problems rather than receive the truth. But strength comes when the Christian resists the lies of the devil on his own volition.

Some never gain strength because they go to counselors, or to fellow Christians, instead of seeking the Lord. Pouring out the problem to a willing listener will only bring temporary relief. There may be temporary joy and victory derived from each counseling session, but the weakness will remain indefinitely, until he begins to exert authority through his own spirit against the enemy.

No preacher or brother or sister in Christ can become strong for you. They can't do your praying, fasting, or resisting of the devil for you. They can give you encouragement and support, but strength comes from doing your own exercise.

Resist the devil!

Preaching Doesn't Make You Strong

The purpose of preaching is not to make you strong, any more than a fitness instructor exhorting you to exercise will make you strong.

The purpose of preaching is to make us clean.

> *'That He might sanctify and **cleanse her** with the washing of water by the word.'*
>
> (Ephesians 5:26)

God has ordained preaching to cleanse us. Preaching is the proclamation and declaration of good news. Hearing an anointed sermon is like taking a shower. The anointed exposition of the word preached, edifies and refreshes and provokes us, and even convicts us, bringing us to repentance. Good preaching should make us uncomfortable and challenge us to seek God with new intensity.

But although it has so many benefits, it will not give us spiritual muscles. That will only come as we **act** upon what we've heard.

Many are under the misconception that if they have a good pastor who can preach well, that is all they need to develop spiritual maturity. Although they may be blessed and edified, growth only comes one way – by exercising what they have heard.

Growing in Biblical understanding and information is not necessarily the same as growing strong in our spirit. Our spirit is strengthened as we develop our relationship with the Lord. If we are not careful, we are growing in head knowledge only, and our spirit is remaining like a shriveled raisin.

'Knowledge puffs up, but love edifies.'

(1 Corinthians 8:1)

*'That He would grant you, according to the riches of His glory, to be **strengthened with might through His Spirit in the inner man.'***

(Ephesians 3:16)

Nothing Makes You Grow Faster Than Seeking the Lord

Human nature, including Christian human nature, gravitates to seeking the advice or opinion of people rather than God. We find it easier to relate to someone we can see, rather than He, Whom we cannot see.

Of course it is not wrong to seek out counsel and encouragement from other people, but true change and growth come when **we** seek the Lord.

Making an investment of time in uninterrupted prayer creates an unexplainable strength to the human spirit. Finding another person to 'unload' the problem on will bring a temporary support and relief, but will not necessarily make you any stronger as a Christian, any more than you would gain strength by watching that person pray.

Satan Has Desired to Sift You Like Wheat, but I Have Prayed For You

Jesus approached Simon at one point to warn him that Satan would desire to prove that he was chaff and not wheat.

'And the Lord said, "Simon, Simon! Indeed, Satan has asked for you, that he may sift you as wheat."'

(Luke 22:31)

From the standpoint of the natural man, we kind of expect Jesus to explain to Simon how He had 'taken care' of Satan and forbidden him to bother Peter any more.

But Jesus says no such thing. Instead He just lets Simon know that He has already prayed for him.

> *'But I have prayed for you, that your faith should not fail; and when you have **returned to Me**, strengthen your brethren.'*
>
> (vs. 32)

What is Jesus saying? He is saying that He won't necessarily 'rescue' us from the harassments of Satan, but He will pray for us!

> *'Therefore He is also able to save to the uttermost those who come to God through Him, since **He always lives to make intercession for them**.'*
>
> (Hebrews 7:25)

The will of God is not to remove all obstacles and put us on easy street, but to make us strong!

It is easy to see where the priorities of Jesus are. First of all we must become strong. Secondly we must be able to strengthen our brothers.

Challenge All Negative Thoughts

Take time, and get off alone in a room without any interruptions. Sit there quietly for twenty or thirty minutes and notice how many negative thoughts enter your mind, and yet go unchallenged.

We must be alert to challenge aggressively all negative thoughts that the enemy would try to plant in our minds. If we challenge them, those thoughts can **never** take root. Usually we are guilty of entertaining such thoughts. But the more you 'feed' a thought, the more it will grow. What you don't 'feed' will starve. We must make a decision to **refuse** to entertain any thoughts that the enemy tries to sow into our minds.

Most of the thoughts the enemy plants in our minds are to discourage us and to rob us of the joy of salvation. He is trying to grow weeds in the fruitful garden that God is cultivating within us. Therefore, it is of utmost importance to resist and challenge **all** thoughts that do not come from the Holy Spirit.

If You Are Resisted, Rejoice!

When the enemy of your soul resists you, it usually means one of two things. Either you are on the verge of a breakthrough, or you are on the right track with God, and the devil is trying to discourage your efforts.

When my wife and I are preparing for a ministry trip, we can usually count on a great deal of resistance. Most of the time, it comes in the form of petty things that become most exasperating and irritating. '... *The little foxes that spoil the vines.*' (Song of Solomon 2:15) The devil is obviously trying to discourage and rob us of joy and victory, because he knows the ministry will do damage to his kingdom.

But we have learned in this to rejoice, because we know that the resistance means we are on the right track. In fact, we usually comment to one another, 'Evidently the meetings are going to be extra good.'

Rather than embracing discouragement, we can rejoice that the devil is worried about us.

It is common when someone is really experiencing satanic opposition, even mental oppression, that that person is usually on the verge of some kind of breakthrough in the near future.

No wonder James tells us to rejoice when we are going through trials!

> '*My brethren, count it all joy when you fall into various trials, knowing that the testing of your faith produces patience.*'
>
> (James 1:2–3)

God is allowing trials to bring forth a permanent result of character in your inner man.

It is similar to taking final exams. Students usually complain when they are facing finals, but the exciting thing is, that if they pass, they will be promoted! They will never again be 'tested' in those areas.

God desires to promote us. He wants to take us to higher and higher levels and dimensions in Him. But no promotion takes place without an exam.

> *'Blessed is the man who endures temptation; for when he has been approved, he will receive the crown of life which the Lord has promised to those who love Him.'*
>
> (James 1:12)

Promotion is on the way!

Chapter 9

Living with a Demand on the Holy Spirit

– We must learn to exert faith that places a demand on the presence of God –

> *'Nevertheless, when the Son of Man comes, will He really find faith on the earth?'*
>
> (Luke 18:8)

A number of months ago, I was seeking the Lord with desperation concerning a certain need in my family. Late one night, just before going to bed, I again prayed with intensity, 'Lord, I have just got to know you are hearing my prayer.'

That night I had a dream. It was very brief. In the dream I was standing in the Oval office facing the President of the United States. The President looked up at me and asked me what I wanted. I told him the need I had. Immediately, he reached behind him and picked up the receiver of his phone (as if to make a call), saying, 'I'll take care of that right now.' I woke up.

As I lay there, pondering the dream, I was so smitten by the telephone the President used. It was so worn and so 'used'. It reminded me of a phone that one would see in an antique store, one that was extremely worn with time and use.

Of course, I knew that the President (in the dream) was representative of the Lord. His prayer 'line' was well-used.

His quickness in reaching for that worn phone was so indicative of His willingness to answer prayer. He was promising me He would take care of my need. And He did! Evidence came in our lives soon thereafter.

There was something very real in that dream that greatly impacted my life. When we pray with desperation, God hears! He promises to 'get right on it.' The worn phone reminded me of how concerned and how willing God is to answer prayer.

If You Are Resisted, You Are Doing Something Right

Last year I was preaching at a church in a small town in the midwestern United States. On the second night of the meetings, I had preached for a while exhorting the people to believe God and to exercise their faith. Suddenly I just felt the Holy Spirit compelling me to walk down among the people. As I did, I felt prompted by the Spirit to go to the last few rows of people. When I walked to the back of the church, I felt such a knowledge in my spirit that the Lord was healing someone of a long standing neck problem.

As I related to the people that God wanted to indeed heal this person who was suffering, an older man acknowledged the fact that it was he. He explained that he had severe arthritis of the neck, and had not been without pain for the past seven years. All of us assembled in the building began to pray and thank God that He was touching this man's body. The service continued for a short duration.

A short time later I went back to the gentleman and asked him how his neck felt. He was excited and exclaimed, that for the first time in seven years, the pain had stopped! He could move his neck in any direction without pain. We all rejoiced, and the Lord continued to move in the meeting, healing and encouraging the people.

The next night more people came than before. Word was spreading that God was moving. After I preached for thirty minutes, I again exhorted the people that God wanted to do things, and to release their faith to Him. As we were all seeking the Lord, and pressing in to Him to meet needs, this same gentleman raised his hand. As I acknowledged him, he requested permission to speak.

He began to testify publicly, repeating what had happened the night before, and explained how he went home very excited that he was finally free of pain. Then he went on to tell us that when he went to bed, the pain started again, and soon the pain became more excruciating than it had ever been in the last seven years.

But God bless this man (I found out later he was a retired minister), he stood his ground. He realized that the devil was indeed trying to rob him of his healing. He did not sleep one wink the entire night, but lay there in such pain, rebuking the powers of darkness.

Finally he could stand it no more. At ten minutes before seven, he got out of bed and walked into his bathroom to the medicine cabinet. He had to have relief. He reached for the potent pain medicine he had been using for the past seven years.

As he reached up to remove the bottle of pills from the shelf, he heard the Holy Spirit say, 'If you don't take those, you just might be healed in ten minutes.' Believing he had heard the lord speak to him, this precious brother put the pills back on the shelf. Exactly ten minutes later, at the stroke of seven o'clock, the pain left. It never returned!

Be Convinced That God Wants to Help You

Thank God this man understood that it was the devil who was trying to steal this wonderful healing from him. And when he had resisted the enemy to the best of his ability, then the Holy Spirit blessed him and he was totally delivered.

Unfortunately, many are robbed of what the Lord desires to do for them because they aren't convinced it is God's will to do it for them in the first place. We must believe the gospel, and cast off **all** feelings of unworthiness.

The devil is a deceiver, and he commonly will slander God to you by saying, 'You didn't have enough faith,' or, 'God is not going to heal you because you haven't lived just right.'

The devil never comes up with anything new. These are the same old lies. I've actually had people who had been touched by God, tell me later that they thought God had changed His mind. That is not possible. He has not changed His mind about Calvary where, with His blood, He purchased us and redeemed us from our sins and, with His scourging, paid for every sickness or disease we could ever face.

But ninety percent of every prayer answered and miracle granted, pivots on whether or not you are convinced that God wants you to have it. Countless people have been robbed by this counter-attack of the devil because they were not totally convinced that God really wanted to do it for them. But the truth is, He has **already** done it, and it is up to us to receive aggressively by faith what He has already accomplished for us.

One way to express it is like this. If you are still trying to persuade God to heal you or to meet a need you have, you haven't yet heard the Gospel! The good news of the Gospel is that Jesus has **already** done it! Prayer isn't asking Him to heal or deliver you. Prayer is finding the release of power and appropriating to your life what He has already accomplished for you!

Don't Lose Heart

An especially enlightening Scripture is in Luke 18 where Jesus taught His disciples to pray and not lose heart.

> *'Then he spoke a parable to them, that men ought to pray and not lose heart.'*
>
> (Luke 18:1)

What significance this has! The first thing that happens when people pray, is they lose heart! The devil resists fervent prayer, so he cruelly hurls the familiar thoughts. 'God isn't interested.' 'It may not be God's will.' 'God has given you this problem to teach you a lesson.' Who feels like praying when you think God doesn't want you to have it?

Don't lose heart! Become one hundred percent convinced

that God wants you to receive a manifestation of your prayer.

Following this statement is the most wonderful parable about a widow who has a need for legal protection. She approaches the unrighteous judge who doesn't have a fear of man or God. Yet the judge ends up granting her request because of her persistent coming to him. She was convinced that he could give it to her, and he did!

> *'There was in a certain city a judge who did not fear God nor regard man. Now there was a widow in that city; and she came to him saying "Avenge me of my adversary." And he would not for a while; but afterward he said within himself, "Though I do not fear God nor regard man, yet because this widow troubles me I will avenge her, lest by her continual coming she weary me."'*
>
> (vs. 2–5)

Look how it reads in the Amplified!

> *'Yet because this widow continues to bother me, I will defend and protect and avenge her; lest she give me intolerable annoyance and wear me out by her continual coming, or at the last she come and rail on me, or assault me, or strangle me.'*
>
> (vs. 5)

The bottom line is that God wants to do things for us, but we must learn to put a **demand** on the Holy Spirit by our **own persistence**.

Notice how Jesus concludes the parable.

> *'Hear what the unjust judge said. And shall God not avenge His own elect who cry out day and night to Him, though he bears long with them? I tell you that He will avenge them speedily. Nevertheless, when the Son of Man comes, will He really find faith on the earth?'*
>
> (vs. 6–8)

The last days' church is going to be accentuated by a

people who know how to press in and touch the heart of God. The Son of man **will** find faith on the earth!

Get in the Spirit

During a difficult time recently, I came to a point of frustration. Despondent, I went into the bedroom and began to pray. I wasn't sure how to pray, so I just kept saying, 'Help me Lord.' Then (being the spiritual giant that I am) I fell asleep. A few minutes later I woke up, and I heard the Holy Spirit say these words to me, 'What you need is not help ...' Then immediately I saw in the Spirit a beautiful white dove, with His wings spread. I knew instantly what the Lord was saying. He was telling me not to pray for help (that prayer was answered when He saved me, and brought me into covenant with Him), rather I was to get on the Dove – to mount up with the wings of the Holy Spirit.

God was gently rebuking me. He was saying to me, 'Get in the Spirit.' His voice was reminding me to live in the realm of the Holy Spirit and lean on Him, minute by minute. In my discouragement, I had begun to depend on the flesh. He had never left, but I had to choose to get on (or stay on) board – to get in the Spirit.

If we're honest with ourselves, we don't like living with a daily dependence on the Holy Spirit. It frustrates our flesh to have to adjust our life style to 'pull' from God twenty-four hours a day.

Like most preachers, I've resisted having to go to the 'trouble' of getting something fresh from God on a frequent basis in order to adequately feed and minister to the saints.

Living with a demand on the Holy Spirit is not some option that God offers us. If we are not hearing what is being declared by the Holy Spirit from the throne of God, then we are not ministering life, but rather that which is synthetic and man-made.

Don't Miss the Adventure!

To best describe the walk in the Spirit, I would have to call it an exciting adventure. Years ago, I heard someone say, 'The walk in the Spirit is like Christmas every day.' I agree. There is nothing in this life more thrilling than to hear from God, and to experience His anointing flowing through your being.

During our first year of pastoring, we bought a beautiful Jewish Synagogue. It had been vacated by its congregation which had dwindled down to such a few that they merged with another group. Although our new church was only a few months old, God miraculously moved and gave us favor with these Jewish people, as well as the bank, and we were able to take possession of the beautiful building in a miraculously short time.

However, after a number of weeks, we quickly realized that there was not adequate parking, as the attendance was rapidly growing. An older man in the church offered his skill of operating a bulldozer, in order to prepare the land to build a parking lot. However, in order to utilize this man's abilities, we needed a bulldozer as well as a dump truck, to haul the excess dirt away.

Consequently, we prayed, we looked through the yellow pages, and we asked around, but we soon found that the prices were astronomical. But then in desperation, we not only prayed, we **listened**. And as we listened, the Holy Spirit, in His faint but familiar voice, simply told us to make it known at the following mid-week service, that we needed the temporary use of a dump truck and a bulldozer.

Even as the Lord told us this simple thing to ask, it was difficult to submit our brains to the idea. It seemed easier to the flesh to somehow raise the money and have it done professionally. Besides we knew everyone in our congregation, and we knew no one had access to a bulldozer or a dump truck. We tried to let God in on that information, but He paid no attention. Finally, by the grace of God, we obeyed. At the midweek service there turned out to be a poor attendance, with more women than men present. (It seems that when God moves, He likes to reduce the odds. It is obvious that He receives more glory when things look impossible.) At an opportune break in the service, I reluctantly made the announcement, convinced that I hadn't heard from God. But as quickly as I stated the church's need for the dump truck and bulldozer, a young man in his early twenties sitting in the back, stood up. To our amazement, he exclaimed, 'I have a small business, and I own a dump truck and a bulldozer that you are welcome to use. I'll bring them by in the morning.'

The young man was a visitor, had never been in our church before, and he did not return, with the exception of one Sunday night, several months later. The night he returned, we prayed with him and he received the Holy Spirit. Soon afterwards he moved away to another city.

How easy it would have been to ignore the Holy Spirit, and strive within our minds to somehow meet the need we had. But the Holy Spirit had the wisdom, as well as the ability, to nudge that young man to be in our service that one time. God knows what He is doing, and He **is** the head of the church.

That's where our problem lies; we do not see Jesus as the Head. We'd rather depend on our own heads. Talk about small thinking!

If we had listened to our own heads, it would have cost us a great deal of money, and the exertion of a lot of flesh to raise the money. Most importantly, the Lord would not have received the glory that He did by sovereignly sending the young man to our service that Thursday night.

Get in the Spirit, or You'll Give Your Opinion

In counseling situations, it is so crucial to **hear what the Spirit is saying** to the individual in need. What a temptation it is to toss out my opinion to that person who is seeking help. When people come for help, the last thing they need is another opinion. Rather than give my opinion, I have to put a demand on God by choosing to listen to Him in that specific situation.

I have found that praying in the Spirit, even for a few seconds, will clear my own mind and pave the way for me to hear what the Lord is saying to that particular person. He will often drop in a phrase, or give an immediate impression, which always proves to be something that will simplify and clarify the situation. The Holy Spirit is the best psychiatrist, and He can quickly diagnose the problem. The good news is that He is available at all times!

The Holy Spirit is amazing. He abides with the believer twenty-four hours a day, every day. He is our access to all the wisdom and knowledge we will ever need.

Don't Go by Feelings?

A common phrase among many Christians is, 'Now you can't go by feelings.' I boldly disagree. It is possible to feel the presence of the Lord. The precious person of the Holy Spirit has feelings. As we walk in unity with Him, He lets us feel what He feels. When He is grieved, we can feel it. When He bears witness to truth, we can feel it. When He checks our spirit, we can feel it. Jesus was grieved in His spirit. He perceived by the Spirit. He rejoiced in the Spirit.

While we do have to be on guard from being on an emotional roller-coaster, we **can** feel what God feels. Emotions and feelings are not necessarily the same thing. Feelings are often intuitive. Emotions are far different from feeling the presence of the Lord (or His absence) in our spirit.

It has helped me to realize that the Holy Spirit is a very tangible and approachable Person. One Scripture that makes this plain is 1 John 2:27, where John describes the anointing.

> *'But the anointing which you have received from Him abides in you, and you do not need that anyone teach you; but as the same anointing teaches you concerning all things, and is true, and is not a lie, and just as it has taught you, you will abide in Him.'*

> (1 John 2:27)

The word 'anointing' is the Greek word, chrisma, which means an unguent or smearing of thick oil. This smearing of oil can be felt on the human spirit. When the Spirit bears witness to truth, the human spirit 'feels' the anointing oil. Likewise, when the Spirit is grieved, the human spirit 'feels' the dryness or lack of anointing oil.

Obviously, it would be wrong to base everything we do on feelings of emotion. But the Holy Spirit is a Person, and we can feel what He feels. We can be in tune with His feelings concerning matters we are seeking Him on.

To be without feelings would be to live in total darkness of what the Holy Spirit is saying in our everyday lives.

The Son Can Do Nothing of Himself

We need to relearn a lot of things. The first thing is that we can accomplish nothing for the kingdom of God in the power of our flesh. But the exciting thing is when we admit that we can do nothing, we leave ourselves wide open and available for the Holy Spirit to initiate His commands in our lives.

It is not enough to learn the lingo, we must **know** the mind of the Spirit.

Jesus lived in total dependence on the Father. He stated that plainly.

> *'Most assuredly, I say to you, the Son can do nothing of Himself, but what He sees the Father do; for whatever He does, the Son also in like manner.'*
>
> (John 5:19)

> *'Though He was a Son, yet He learned obedience by the things which He suffered.'*
>
> (Hebrews 5:8)

The deplorable thing is that leadership has taught people the right lingo, and the right doctrine, but no one seems to know **how to hear** from God. Yet, what can be more basic to walking after the Spirit, than to hear the voice of God? Grievously, we have taught people to look outwardly for the oracle of what God is saying rather than inwardly, as He communicates by His Spirit to our inner man. We are guilty of encouraging people to accept confirmation and affirmation from the leading Christian magazine, denominational head-quarters, or the so-called leading authorities on the Holy Spirit, rather than to listen to the voice of the Lord on the inside of them.

There is not necessarily anything wrong with hearing what God is saying through leading people and magazines and organizations, but the problem is that we have taught people to **substitute** that for recognizing the voice of the Spirit within their own inner man. This is new-covenant living. *'All shall know me from the least of them to the greatest.'* (Hebrews 8:10)

Learn by Doing, Not by Hearing

My wife was seeking the Lord one day, and asked Him what makes our spirit grow and mature. He spoke back to her three answers, 'Dedicated, and consecrated prayer.' 'The light of revelation.' 'Giving out.'

The Holy Spirit says volumes to us in a few words. The meaning of what He was saying to her became obvious. Consecrated prayer **builds** our spirit. The spirit of revelation **feeds** our spirit. Giving out, **exercises** our spirit.

That is precisely why there are so many **dwarf** Christians today. Nothing makes a Christian grow faster than listening to the voice of the Spirit within him, and obeying that Voice. People have not grown spiritually oftentimes, because they only know what leaders and denominations and magazines are saying, not necessarily what the Spirit is saying.

Christian growth doesn't come by hearing, but by doing. For example, to learn how to operate a computer, the fastest way is by sitting down and doing it. You can listen to people tell you how it works or how to do commands, up to a point. But until you actually go through the commands and use the computer for yourself, you will be a novice. Merely listening to others explain it is extremely limiting. Young people are quite adept at computers, because they are eager to just sit down and do it. Equally, they have nothing to unlearn. They just begin operating one, and quickly figure it out. It is amazing how quickly they catch on, just by doing it. So too, our growth in spiritual things comes by active obedience.

The writer of Hebrews addresses this lack of growth among Christians.

> *'For by this time you ought to be teachers, you need someone to teach you again the first principles of the oracles of God; and you have come to need milk and not solid food. For everyone who partakes only of milk is unskilled in the word of righteousness, for he is a babe. But solid food belongs to those who are of full age, that is, those who by reason of use have their senses exercised to discern both good and evil.*

(Hebrews 5:12–14)

When the writer talks about discerning both good and evil; it doesn't mean discerning good **from** evil. Rather it means discerning **good** from **God** and **evil** from **carnal**.

It is not too difficult to discern good from evil. What is difficult is to discern that which is **seemingly good from what is being spoken by God**. Christians must walk with this discernment. Not everything that looks good and sounds good is necessarily something that God is saying to do.

Some things are not necessarily evil (as blatant sin would be) but they are evil in the sense that they are only the product of our own thoughts and **not God-breathed and initiated**. This would include **any** impulsive decisions made concerning the kingdom of God, without consulting the Holy Spirit. So many endeavours are done 'for' God, that were never initiated 'by' God.

Living by the Oracle

Israel received an awesome and exciting promise from God.

> *'I am the Lord your God, Who brought you out of the land of Egypt; Open your mouth wide, and I will fill it.'*
> (Psalm 81:10)

This was new covenant living! Out of relationship, the covenant would work. God would literally place His words in their mouths as they walked before Him.

God's plan was that He would put a living oracle in their mouths that would give them total access to His awesome power, if they would seek Him.

But Israel rejected this type of living.

> '*But My people would not heed My voice. And Israel would have none of Me.*'

(vs. 11)

Notice He did not say they refused to be religious or read the Bible, but they refused to accept an intimate relationship with God, Himself.

This is the precise place where the rubber hits the road, so to speak. dependent living, trusting the Holy Spirit to communicate to you, is hard on the flesh. Our flesh always chooses the religious, formula-ridden way. To the flesh it seems difficult to live dependent on the Holy Spirit, because we **think** we want independence from the responsibility of having to 'tune in' or pay attention to the Spirit of God.

But the good news of the new covenant is that God has already taken the word out of the contract. It is a foolproof covenant. It is a covenant dependent on the faithfulness of God, and not on our fleshly determination.

For example, as we read on to the following verses, it becomes more obvious. Listening to God is protection from our enemies!

> '*Oh, that My people would **listen to Me**, that Israel would walk in My ways! I would soon subdue their enemies, and turn My hand against their adversaries.*'

(vs. 13–14)

In covenant living, God promises to overthrow all our enemies with no effort on our part. All that He requires of us is that we walk with an open and transparent heart before Him.

There is no big 'devil' problem if we recognize that this is a listening covenant. Instead, **we** are to become the devil's problem! Somehow, it appeals to the flesh to spend more time fighting the devil than spending quality time in the presence of the Lord, and discerning His mind in every situation.

Avoid Going Through the Motions

During my first few years as a Spirit-filled Christian, I was so blessed to be a part of a large inter-denominational church in Kansas City called the Evangelistic Center. The worship in the Spirit was wonderful, as the congregation would often sing in the Spirit at length, and God was allowed to be in control. Many wonderful manifestations of the Holy Spirit would transpire.

Yet, even in such an awesome atmosphere (the presence of the Lord was indescribable) I would notice that there would be a certain percentage of people who never changed. I asked others, who were more mature in the Lord, about my observation. The answer was always the same. There are some who let the Holy Spirit work and refine them; there are others who refuse.

If you are even remotely open to the Lord, you cannot consistently be in an atmosphere such as that, where the Lord is present, without letting Him bring change in your heart, motives and attitude.

However, there are always people who think they can fake God out. There are always those in the assembly of the saints who are still doing their own thing. Outwardly they are moving in the things of God, but inwardly they stubbornly maintain ownership of their own wills.

> *'The haters of the Lord would pretend submission to Him, but their fate would endure forever.'*
>
> (Psalm 81:15)

True spiritual worship **always** brings you to a point of confrontation. That is why some people are extremely uncomfortable in a church that really has true worship. There is something about worship that touches the heart of God, and His light is manifested. Once that light begins to come, it quickly searches the soul. Then the 'worshipper' has to make a **decision** to move on with God, and confront the area the Lord is shining light on, or he will simply stunt his spiritual growth and perhaps go to another church. Most often the church he chooses will be one that doesn't require people to enter the presence of God. Even though doctrinally the 'new' church believes in the power of the Holy Spirit, the leadership has compromised where it comes to pure worship, and thus the presence of God is rarely manifested. Naturally, people can be pretty comfortable in that atmosphere, as there will not be the manifest presence of the Lord there to convict them.

> '... *I know your works, that you have a name that you are alive, but you are dead.*'
>
> (Revelation 3:1)

It is not enough to have knowledge, we must be identified with Him. That is where the life is. There is nothing more exciting or fruitful than living with a demand on the Holy Spirit.

He's available twenty-four hours!

Order Form

★ Cut out and send in with your order ★

Please send me:

_____ copies of ***Breaking the Bondage Barrier – Taking the Limits off God*** ($7.00 each)

_____ copies of ***You Can't Use Me Today, Lord ... I Don't Feel Spiritual*** ($6.00 each)

_____ copies of ***Enjoying God and Other Rare Events*** ($3.00 each)

_____ copies of ***Don't Talk to Me Now, Lord ... I'm Trying to Pray*** ($4.00 each)

_____ copies of ***Listening to the Holy Spirit – Expecting the Miraculous*** ($5.00 each)
   ☆ This is a revised printed edition of *Don't Talk to Me Now, Lord ... I'm Trying to Pray!* ☆

_____ copies of ***Medicine for the Mind*** pamphlet (5 for $1.00)

_____ Catalog of Cassette Tapes

I am enclosing _____ plus $2.00 for postage and handling. (Overseas orders please add an additional 20% of total)

Mr/Mrs/Miss _____

Address _____

_____ City _____

State _____ Zipcode _____

Country _____

Order from: **Steve Sampson, PO Box 36324, Birmingham, AL 35236, USA.**